Number Words

1. Trace the numbers and the number words.
    Draw a line to match the numbers to the counters.

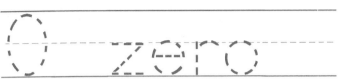

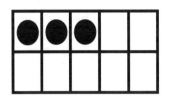

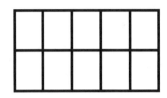

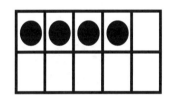

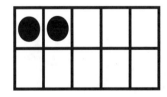

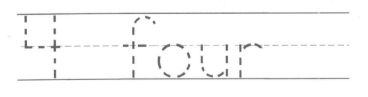

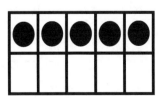

2. Trace the numbers and the number words.
   Draw a line to match the numbers to the counters.

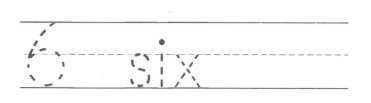

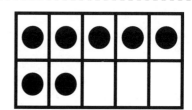

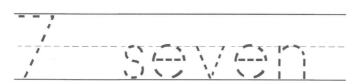

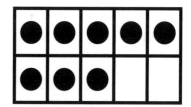

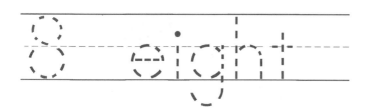

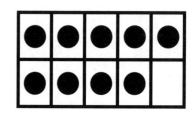

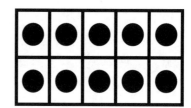

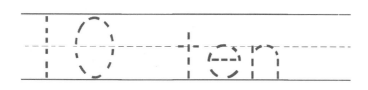

3. How old are you?

_____

- -

_____

Numbers

1. Trace the numbers. Draw ● to show each numbers.

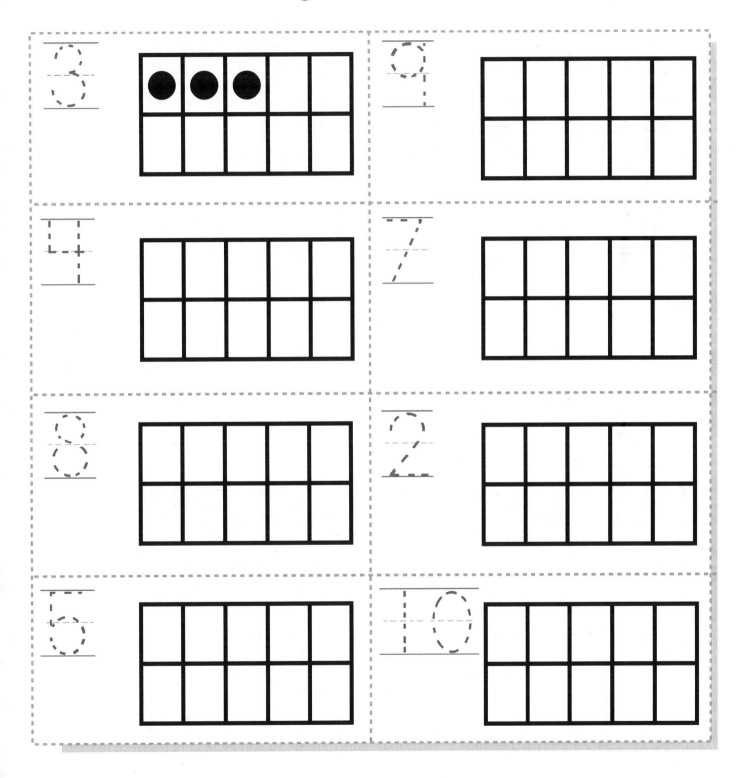

Using Ten-Frames to Count to 10

1. How many counters are there?

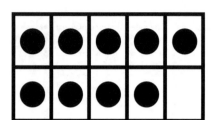 _____

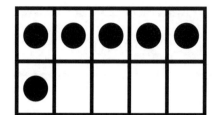 _____

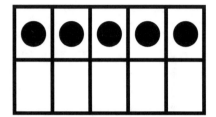 _____

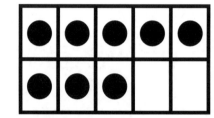 _____

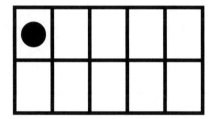 _____

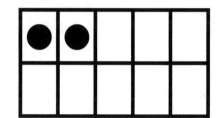 _____

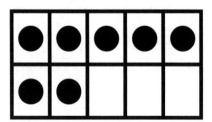 _____

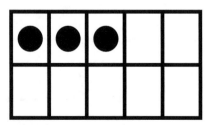 _____

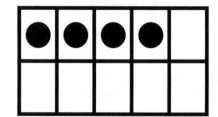 _____

Comparing Numbers from 1 to 10

Compare numbers by counting.

3 is **less than** 5

4 is **greater than** 2

9 is **equal to** 9

1. Compare the numbers. Write the words **greater than, less than,** or **equal to**.

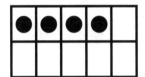 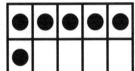

4 is _____ 6

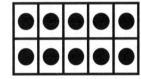 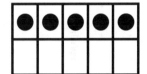

10 is _____ 5

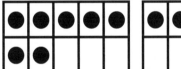 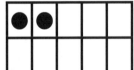

7 is _____ 2

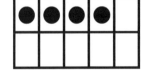 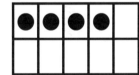

4 is _____ 4

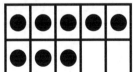 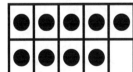

8 is _____ 9

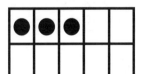 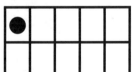

3 is _____ 1

Numbers and Number Words

1. Match the number to the number word.

0	nine
1	six
2	eight
3	zero
4	one
5	ten
6	two
7	three
8	four
9	five
10	seven

BRAIN STRETCH

1. What is the number word for 4? Circle the correct answer.

three   four   two

2. What is the number word for 8? Circle the correct answer.

five   seven   eight

Number Word Search

1. Circle the correct words in the word search. Cross words off the list when you find them.

s	z	e	r	o	o	n	e
e	t	t	f	n	i	n	e
v	w	e	o	f	h	o	s
e	o	n	u	q	t	b	i
n	k	z	r	e	k	l	x
a	b	e	i	g	h	t	v
s	t	h	r	e	e	n	x
t	p	w	f	i	v	e	v

one   four   seven   ten

two   five   eight   zero

three   six   nine

Counting, Then Writing the Number

1. Look at the picture. How many are there of each creature? Write the number in the box below the creature.

More, Fewer, and Less

1. Circle the correct set. Write **more** or **fewer**.

a) Circle the set that has **fewer**.

1 is **fewer** than 2.

b) Circle the set that has **more** creatures.

_____ is _____ than _____.

c) Circle the set that has **fewer** creatures.

_____ is _____ than _____.

d) Circle the set that has **more** creatures.

_____ is _____ than _____.

2. Draw to show more or fewer shapes.

Show **2** more.

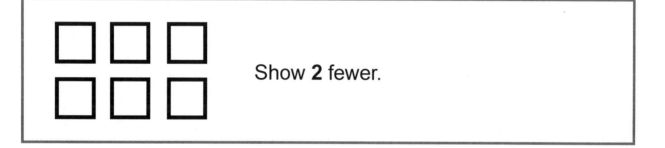

Show **2** fewer.

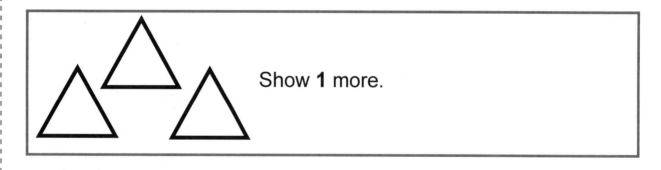

Show **1** more.

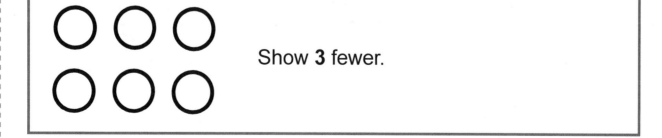

Show **3** fewer.

Using Ten-Frames to Count to 20

1. How many counters are there?

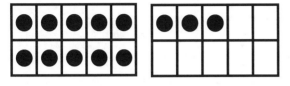

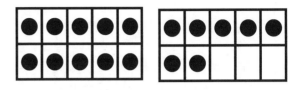

13 _____

_____

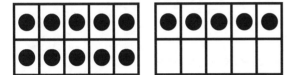

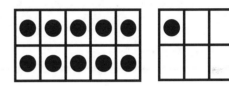

_____

_____

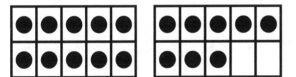

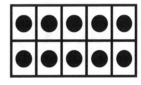 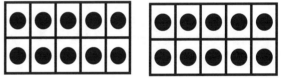

_____

_____

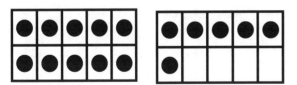

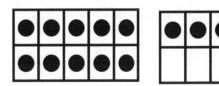 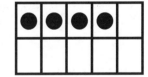

_____

_____

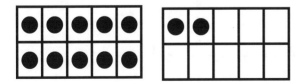

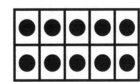 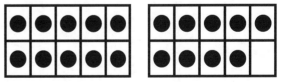

_____

_____

2. Draw s in the ten-frames to equal the number.

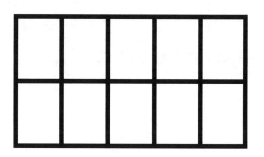
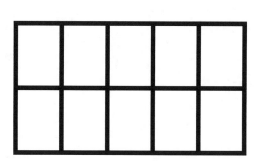

15

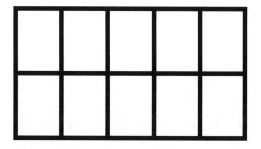
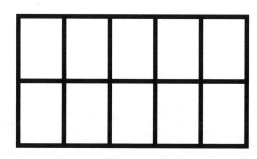

11

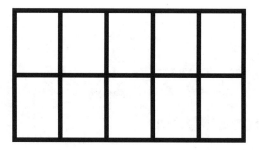
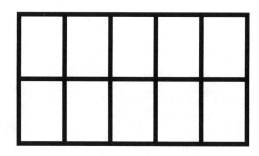

17

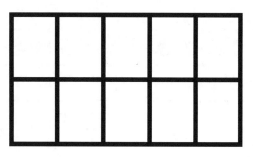
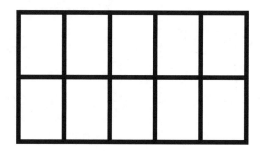

12

3. Draw ●s in the ten-frames to equal the number.

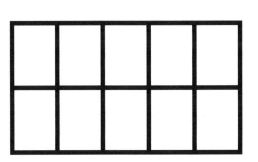 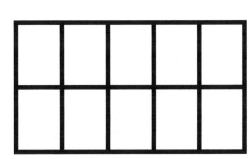

20

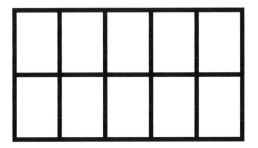 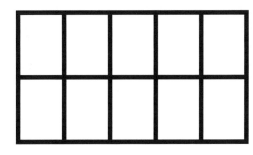

14

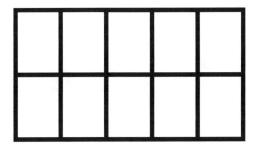 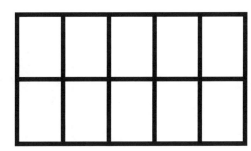

19

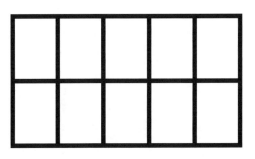 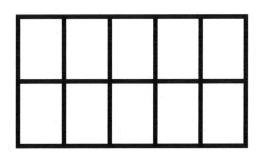

11

4. Draw ●s in the ten-frames to equal the number.

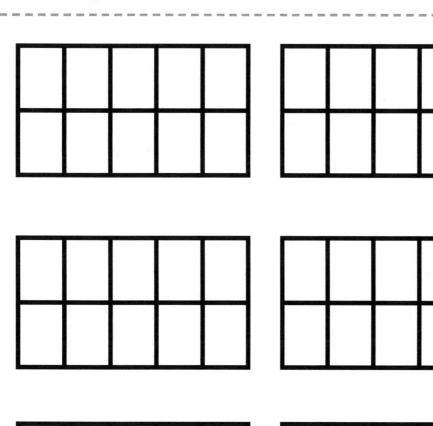

16

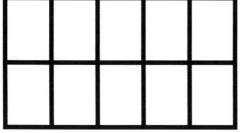 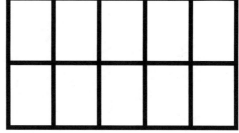

18

13

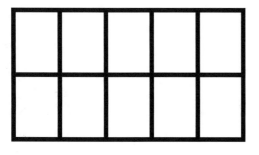 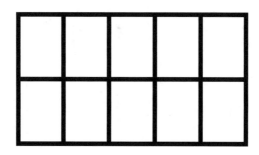

10

Counting from 0 to 20

Connect the dots by counting from 0 to 20. Count out loud.

1. Name this creature. _____

2. What makes the creature special? _____

Ordering Numbers

1. Fill in the missing numbers. Use the number line to help you.

0 1 2 3 4 5 6 7 8 9 10 11 12 13 14 15 16 17 18 19 20

Just before: __10__ , 11, 12

Just before: _____ , 4, 5

Just after: 13, 14, _____

Just before and after: _____ , 16, _____

Between: 5, _____ , 7

Just after: 16, 17, _____

Just before and after: _____ , 8, _____

Between: 12, _____ , 14

Just after: 15, 16, _____

Just before: _____ , 17, 18

BRAIN STRETCH

Name the number just after 14, 15, and 16. Circle your answer.

13   10   17

Counting to 50

Connect the dots to count to 50. Count out loud.

1. Name the creature. _____

2. What makes the creature special? _____

Counting to 100

1. Fill in the missing numbers on the chart.

1	2	3	4	5	6		8	9	10
11	12	13	14		16	17	18		20
	22	23		25	26		28	29	
	32	33	34	35	36	37	38	39	40
41		43		45		47	48		50
51	52		54		56	57		59	
61			64		66		68	69	70
71	72	73	74	75		77		79	80
81	82	83		85		87	88	89	90
	92	93	94	95	96	97			100

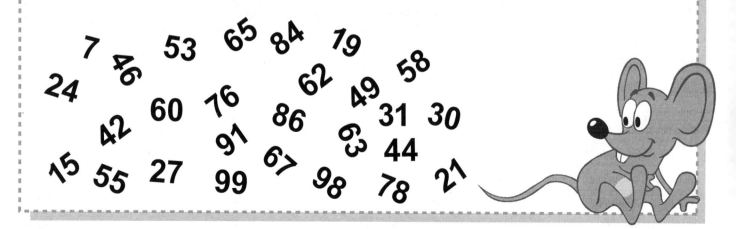

Counting by 2s to 100

1. Count out loud by 2s to 100. Connect the dots.

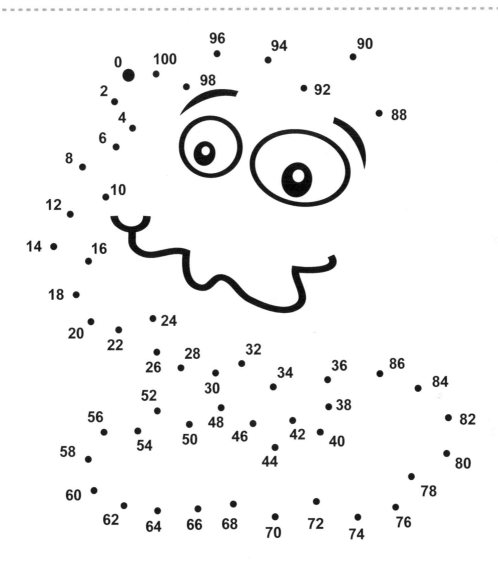

Name the creature. _____

Counting by 5s to 100

1. Count out loud by 5s to 100. Connect the dots.

Name the creature. _____

BRAIN STRETCH

Count by 5s.

| 5 | | | | |

Ordinal Numbers to 10

An ordinal number tells the position of something in a list.

1. Read the ordinal numbers. Underline the part that is the same.

first	second	third	fourth	fifth	sixth	seventh	eighth	ninth	tenth
1st	2nd	3rd	4th	5th	6th	7th	8th	9th	10th

2. Circle the correct answer.

a. The is _____ in line.

b. The is _____ in line.

c. The is _____ in line.

d. The is _____ in line.

e. Who is first?

f. Who is last?

g. Who is between the 3rd and 5th creature?

BRAIN STRETCH

Mark the 2nd creature with an X. Circle the 5th creature.

Groups of Ten

Circle the groups of ten. Count the ones left over. How many in all?

1.

How many groups of 10? __2__   How many left over? __1__   How many in all? __21__

2.

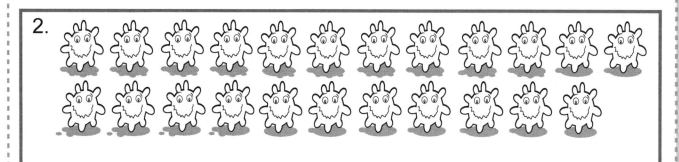

How many groups of 10? _____   How many left over? _____   How many in all? _____

3.

How many groups of 10? _____   How many left over? _____   How many in all? _____

Groups of Ten (continued)

Circle the groups of ten. Count the ones left over. How many in all?

4.

How many groups of 10? _____ How many left over? _____ How many in all? _____

5.

How many groups of 10? _____ How many left over? _____ How many in all? _____

6.

How many groups of 10? _____ How many left over? _____ How many in all? _____

Tens and Ones

Count the tens and ones. Write how many blocks in all.

 Each stack has **10** blocks. Each block is one.

1 ten   + 3 ones   = 13 ones

1.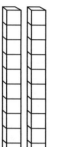

_____ tens + _____ ones =

_____ ones

2.

_____ tens + _____ ones =

_____ ones

3.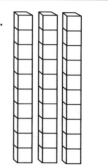

_____ tens + _____ ones =

_____ ones

4.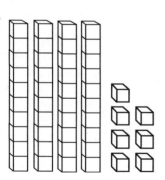

_____ tens + _____ ones =

_____ ones

5.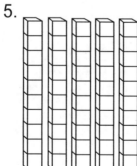

_____ tens + _____ ones =

_____ ones

6.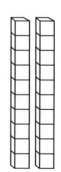

_____ tens + _____ ones =

_____ ones

Count the tens and ones. Write how many blocks in all.

7.

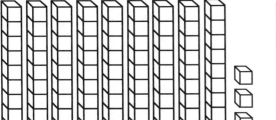

_____ tens + _____ ones =

_____ ones

8.

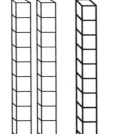

_____ tens + _____ ones =

_____ ones

9.

_____ tens + _____ ones =

_____ ones

10.

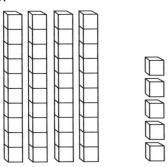

_____ tens + _____ ones =

_____ ones

11.

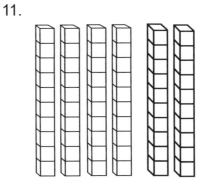

_____ tens + _____ ones =

_____ ones

12.

_____ tens + _____ ones =

_____ ones

BRAIN STRETCH

Draw the blocks for 2 tens and 3 ones.
What is the number?

Addition Stories

Write the number sentence.

1.

_____ **+** _____ **=** _____

2.

_____ **+** _____ **=** _____

3.

_____ **+** _____ **=** _____

4.

_____ **+** _____ **=** _____

5.

_____ **+** _____ **=** _____

6.

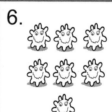

_____ **+** _____ **=** _____

7.

_____ **+** _____ **=** _____

8.

_____ **+** _____ **=** _____

Addition Stories (continued)

Write the number sentence.

9.

_____ + _____ = _____

10.

_____ + _____ = _____

11.

_____ + _____ = _____

12.

_____ + _____ = _____

13.

_____ + _____ = _____

14.

_____ + _____ = _____

15.

_____ + _____ = _____

16.

_____ + _____ = _____

Write the number sentence.

17.

_____ + _____ = _____

18.

_____ + _____ = _____

19.

_____ + _____ = _____

20.

_____ + _____ = _____

21.

_____ + _____ = _____

22.

_____ + _____ = _____

23.

_____ + _____ = _____

24.

_____ + _____ = _____

Adding 1 or 2 by Counting On

Add 1 by counting on.

4 + 1 = _____

Start with the greater number.
Count on by 1.

  4   5

Stop when 1 finger is up.

4 + 1 = __5__

Add 2 by counting on.

4 + 2 = _____

Start with the greater number.
Count on by 2.

  4   5   6

Stop when 2 fingers are up.

4 + 2 = __6__

1. Count on to add.

3 + 1 = _____ 3, _____	7 + 2 = _____ 7, _____, _____
5 + 1 = _____ 5, _____	1 + 2 = _____ 1, _____, _____
16 + 1 = _____ 16, _____	18 + 2 = _____ 18, _____, _____

2. Count on to add.

9 + 1 = _____ 9, _____	3 + 2 = _____ 3, _____, _____
6 + 1 = _____ 6, _____	14 + 2 = _____ 14, _____, _____
1 + 1 = _____ 1, _____	8 + 2 = _____ 8, _____, _____
7 + 1 = _____ 7, _____	5 + 2 = _____ 5, _____, _____
8 + 1 = _____ 8, _____	0 + 2 = _____ 0, _____, _____
17 + 1 = _____ 17, _____	13 + 2 = _____ 13, _____, _____

Addition Doubles

Write the number sentence.

1. ● + ●   _____ + _____ = _____

2. ● ● + ● ●   _____ + _____ = _____

3. ● ● ● + ● ● ●   _____ + _____ = _____

4. ● ● + ● ●   _____ + _____ = _____

5. ● ● ● + ● ● ●   _____ + _____ = _____

6. ● ● ● + ● ● ●   _____ + _____ = _____

Using a Number Line to Add

Use a number line to add.

6 + 3 = ___9___

SAY: 7, 8, 9

Mark a dot at 6.
Draw 3 jumps to count on.
Stop at 9.

1. Use the number line to add. Mark a dot to show where to start.
   Next, count on by drawing the jumps. Write the answer.

2 + 6 = ___

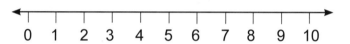

6 + 4 = ___

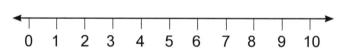

1 + 8 = ___

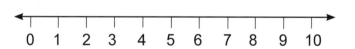

2 + 7 = ___

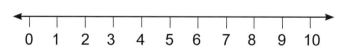

2. Use the number line to add by counting on. Mark a dot to show where to start. Next, draw the jumps. Write the answer.

0 + 5 = _____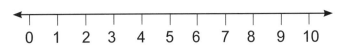

7 + 2 = _____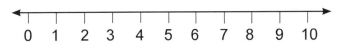

5 + 1 = _____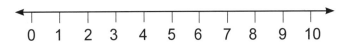

2 + 3 = _____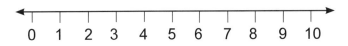

4 + 4 = _____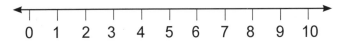

3 + 5 = _____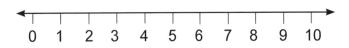

5 + 4 = _____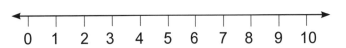

Numbers Can Be Added in Any Order

1. Use the ten-frames to show adding numbers in two ways. Use two different colours. Then, write the answers.

5 + 2 = 7
2 + 5 = 7

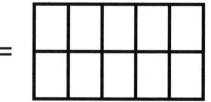

6 + 3 = ____
3 + 6 = ____

2 + 4 = ____
4 + 2 = ____

1 + 7 = ____
7 + 1 = ____

4 + 5 = ____
5 + 4 = ____

8 + 2 = ____
2 + 8 = ____

2. Use the ten-frames to show adding numbers in two ways.
   Use two different colours. Then, write the answers.

6 + 4 = _____
4 + 6 = _____

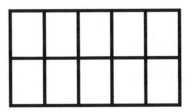

7 + 2 = _____
2 + 7 = _____

3 + 4 = _____
4 + 3 = _____

1 + 9 = _____
9 + 1 = _____

1 + 2 = _____
2 + 1 = _____

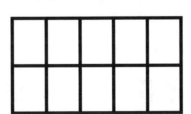

Make your own question.
Use numbers that are
less than 10.

_____ + _____ = _____ + _____

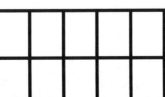
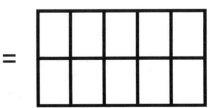

Making 10 to Add

Use a group of 10 to help you add.

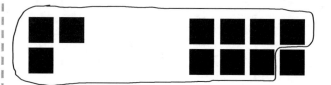

3 + 8 = 10 + _1_ = _11_

Circle 10. There is 1 more block.
Use 10 to add.

5 + 7 = 10 + ___ = ___

7 + 7 = 10 + ___ = ___

4 + 9 = 10 + ___ = ___

5 + 8 = 10 + ___ = ___

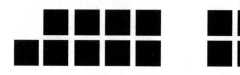

9 + 6 = 10 + ___ = ___

Making Addition Sentences

1. Show three ways to make each number.
   Use two colours to colour the blocks.

___ + ___ = 4

___ + ___ = 4

___ + ___ = 4

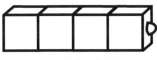
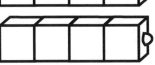
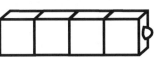

___ + ___ = 7

___ + ___ = 7

___ + ___ = 7

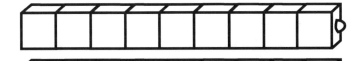

___ + ___ = 9

___ + ___ = 9

___ + ___ = 9

___ + ___ = 11

___ + ___ = 11

___ + ___ = 11

Making Addition Sentences (continued)

2. Show three ways to make each number.
   Use two colours to colour the blocks.

___ + ___ = 10

___ + ___ = 10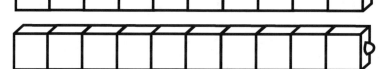

___ + ___ = 10

___ + ___ = 6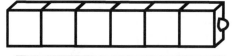

___ + ___ = 6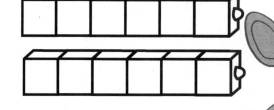

___ + ___ = 6

___ + ___ = 12

___ + ___ = 12

___ + ___ = 12

___ + ___ = 8

___ + ___ = 8

___ + ___ = 8

Subtraction Stories

Count the creatures, then take away. Write the number sentence.

1.

_____4_____ – _____3_____ = _____1_____

2.

_____ – _____ = _____

3.

_____ – _____ = _____

4.

_____ – _____ = _____

5.

_____ – _____ = _____

6.

_____ – _____ = _____

7.

_____ – _____ = _____

8.

_____ – _____ = _____

Subtraction Stories (continued)

Count the creatures, then take away. Write the number sentence.

9. 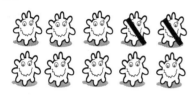	10. 
_____ – _____ = _____	_____ – _____ = _____

11. 	12. 
_____ – _____ = _____	_____ – _____ = _____

13. 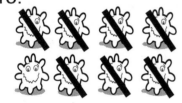	14. 
_____ – _____ = _____	_____ – _____ = _____

15. 	16. 
_____ – _____ = _____	_____ – _____ = _____

Subtraction Stories (continued)

Count the creatures, then take away. Write the number sentence.

17.

_____ – _____ = _____

18.

_____ – _____ = _____

19.

_____ – _____ = _____

20.

_____ – _____ = _____

21.

_____ – _____ = _____

22.

_____ – _____ = _____

23.

_____ – _____ = _____

24.

_____ – _____ = _____

Subtracting 1 or 2 by Counting Back

Subtract 1 by counting back.	**Subtract 2 by counting back.**
3 – 1 = _____	5 – 2 = _____
Count back from the first number.	Count back from the first number.
Count out loud.	Count out loud.
3 2	5 4 3
Stop when 1 finger is up.	Stop when 2 fingers are up.
3 – 1 = __2__	5 – 2 = __3__

1. Subtract by counting back.

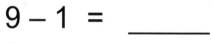

9 – 1 = _____ 9, _____	8 – 2 = _____ 8, _____ , _____
7 – 1 = _____ 7, _____	4 – 2 = _____ 4, _____ , _____
5 – 1 = _____ 5, _____	6 – 2 = _____ 6, _____ , _____
18 – 1 = _____ 18, _____	17 – 2 = _____ 17, _____ , _____

Subtracting 1 or 2 by Counting Back (continued)

2. Count back to subtract.

$4 - 1 =$ _____ 4, _____	$9 - 2 =$ _____ 9, _____, _____
$2 - 1 =$ _____ 2, _____	$10 - 2 =$ _____ 10, _____, _____
$6 - 1 =$ _____ 6, _____	$7 - 2 =$ _____ 7, _____, _____
$8 - 1 =$ _____ 8, _____	$12 - 2 =$ _____ 12, _____, _____
$13 - 1 =$ _____ 13, _____	$3 - 2 =$ _____ 3, _____, _____
$15 - 1 =$ _____ 15, _____	$11 - 2 =$ _____ 11, _____, _____
$12 - 1 =$ _____ 12, _____	$19 - 2 =$ _____ 19, _____, _____

Using a Number Line to Subtract

Use a number line to subtract.

$8 - 4 =$ ___4___

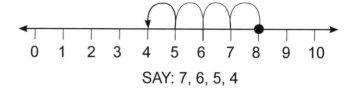

SAY: 7, 6, 5, 4

Mark a dot at 8.
Draw 4 jumps to count back.
Stop at 4.

1. Use the number line to subtract. Mark a dot to show where you start. Next count back by drawing the jumps. Write the answer.

$9 - 6 =$ _____

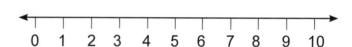

$6 - 3 =$ _____

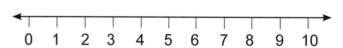

$4 - 2 =$ _____

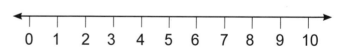

$7 - 1 =$ _____

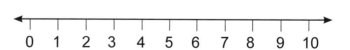

Using a Number Line to Subtract (continued)

2. Use the number line to subtract. Mark a dot to show where you start. Next count back by drawing the jumps. Write the answer.

9 – 5 = _____

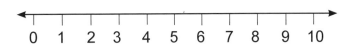

5 – 3 = _____

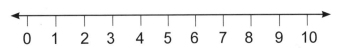

7 – 2 = _____

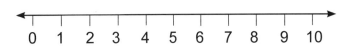

8 – 1 = _____

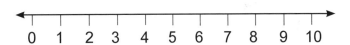

10 – 4 = _____

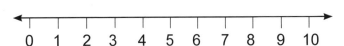

3 – 3 = _____

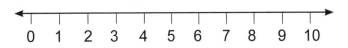

9 – 8 = _____

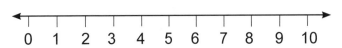

Making Subtraction Sentences

1. Cross out the blocks you want to take away. Colour the blocks left. Complete the subtraction sentence.

9 – ___ = ___

9 – ___ = ___

9 – ___ = ___

6 – ___ = ___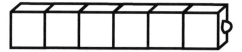

6 – ___ = ___

6 – ___ = ___

4 – ___ = ___

4 – ___ = ___

4 – ___ = ___

10 – ___ = ___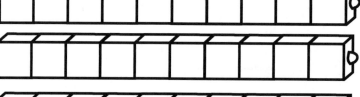

10 – ___ = ___

10 – ___ = ___

Making Subtraction Sentences (continued)

2. Cross out the blocks you want to take away. Colour the blocks left.
   Complete the subtraction sentence.

7 − ___ = ___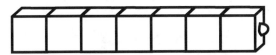

7 − ___ = ___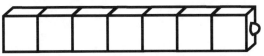

7 − ___ = ___

5 − ___ = ___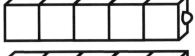

5 − ___ = ___

5 − ___ = ___

8 − ___ = ___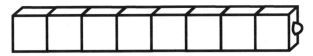

8 − ___ = ___

8 − ___ = ___

12 − ___ = ___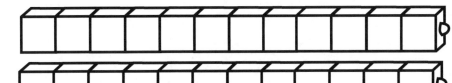

12 − ___ = ___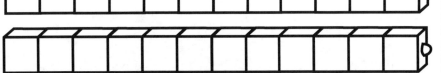

12 − ___ = ___

Sums to 5

1. Complete each addition sentence. Use the key to colour the picture.

Colour Key
0 – red
1 – blue
2 – green
3 – orange
4 – brown
5 – yellow

4 + 1 = _____

2 + 0 = _____

1 + 3 = _____

2 + 2 = _____

1 + 0 = _____

0 + 4 = _____

3 + 1 = _____

5 + 0 = _____

0 + 1 = _____

1 + 4 = _____

3 + 2 = _____

0 + 0 = _____

1 + 1 = _____

2 + 3 = _____

0 + 5 = _____

2 + 1 = _____

4 + 0 = _____

0 + 2 = _____

2. Add.

$$
\begin{array}{r} 4 \\ + 1 \\ \hline \end{array}
\qquad
\begin{array}{r} 2 \\ + 2 \\ \hline \end{array}
\qquad
\begin{array}{r} 0 \\ + 2 \\ \hline \end{array}
$$

$$
\begin{array}{r} 5 \\ + 0 \\ \hline \end{array}
\qquad
\begin{array}{r} 0 \\ + 4 \\ \hline \end{array}
\qquad
\begin{array}{r} 0 \\ + 3 \\ \hline \end{array}
\qquad
\begin{array}{r} 3 \\ + 2 \\ \hline \end{array}
\qquad
\begin{array}{r} 1 \\ + 3 \\ \hline \end{array}
$$

$$
\begin{array}{r} 3 \\ + 0 \\ \hline \end{array}
\qquad
\begin{array}{r} 4 \\ + 0 \\ \hline \end{array}
\qquad
\begin{array}{r} 1 \\ + 4 \\ \hline \end{array}
\qquad
\begin{array}{r} 2 \\ + 3 \\ \hline \end{array}
\qquad
\begin{array}{r} 1 \\ + 1 \\ \hline \end{array}
$$

$$
\begin{array}{r} 0 \\ + 1 \\ \hline \end{array}
\qquad
\begin{array}{r} 2 \\ + 1 \\ \hline \end{array}
\qquad
\begin{array}{r} 3 \\ + 1 \\ \hline \end{array}
\qquad
\begin{array}{r} 1 \\ + 0 \\ \hline \end{array}
\qquad
\begin{array}{r} 1 \\ + 2 \\ \hline \end{array}
$$

Sums to 10

1. Complete each addition sentence. Use the key to colour the picture.

Colour Key
1 – red
2 – blue
3 – green
4 – orange
5 – brown
6 – yellow
7 – purple
8 – pink
9 – grey
10 – black

2 + 1 = _____

1 + 2 = _____

3 + 6 = _____

5 + 2 = _____

6 + 0 = _____

0 + 3 = _____

3 + 4 = _____

1 + 1 = _____

1 + 0 = _____

2 + 2 = _____

1 + 5 = _____

4 + 4 = _____

3 + 1 = _____

2 + 3 = _____

4 + 1 = _____

2 + 5 = _____

6 + 1 = _____

3 + 7 = _____

2. Add.

```
  3        1        5
+ 1      + 1      + 2
____     ____     ____
```

```
  0        5        2        1        0
+ 8      + 0      + 3      + 2      + 10
____     ____     ____     ____     ____
```

```
  4        6        4        7        3
+ 4      + 1      + 2      + 3      + 5
____     ____     ____     ____     ____
```

```
  2        3        4        2        4
+ 5      + 6      + 1      + 2      + 5
____     ____     ____     ____     ____
```

BRAIN STRETCH

7 + 1 + 0 =   3 + 5 + 2 =

3. Add.

```
    5           2           8
  + 5         + 6         + 2
  _____       _____       _____


    2           8           3           4           3
  + 2         + 1         + 3         + 4         + 0
  _____       _____       _____       _____       _____


    3           2           0           1          10
  + 6         + 3         + 9         + 5         + 0
  _____       _____       _____       _____       _____


    1           5           4           2           1
  + 4         + 4         + 3         + 8         + 7
  _____       _____       _____       _____       _____
```

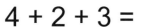

BRAIN STRETCH

4 + 2 + 3 =   5 + 1 + 2 =

4. Add.

7	5	5
+ 1	+ 1	+ 2

8	5	2	1	6
+ 2	+ 3	+ 3	+ 4	+ 4

1	4	9	2	6
+ 3	+ 2	+ 1	+ 2	+ 2

2	1	3	2	3
+ 1	+ 8	+ 2	+ 7	+ 6

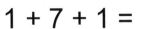

BRAIN STRETCH

1 + 7 + 1 =   3 + 5 + 1 =

5. Add.

| 5 | 2 | 7 |
| + 4 | + 6 | + 2 |

| 2 | 6 | 3 | 4 | 5 |
| + 4 | + 1 | + 7 | + 5 | + 0 |

| 6 | 2 | 1 | 4 | 1 |
| + 3 | + 5 | + 5 | + 4 | + 1 |

| 5 | 8 | 2 | 3 | 3 |
| + 5 | + 1 | + 8 | + 3 | + 1 |

BRAIN STRETCH

8 + 1 + 0 =   2 + 2 + 4 =

Sums to 20

1. Add. Use the number line or counters to help you add.
    Hint: Start with the greater number.

0 1 2 3 4 5 6 7 8 9 10 11 12 13 14 15 16 17 18 19 20

6 + 6	9 + 4	10 + 2	8 + 6	11 + 3
9 + 2	15 + 0	12 + 3	8 + 7	7 + 7
10 + 10	9 + 10	11 + 1	10 + 4	4 + 7
9 + 5	6 + 7	9 + 9	8 + 5	10 + 3

Number Sentence Match

1. Match the number sentence to the answer.

3 + 5 =	12
1 + 0 =	8
2 + 2 =	6
4 + 2 =	5
5 + 5 =	9
2 + 1 =	2
8 + 3 =	4
6 + 6 =	10
7 + 2 =	1
5 + 2 =	3
1 + 1 =	7
3 + 2 =	11

Story Problems

1. Solve the story problems.

There are **3**  on the ground.
Then **2** more 🐛 come.

How many 🐛 are there in all?

_____ ☐ _____ = _____

There are **4**  on the flower.
1 more 🐝 comes.

How many 🐝 are there in total?

_____ ☐ _____ = _____

There are **2**  on the branch.
5 more 🐔 come.

How many 🐔 are there altogether?

_____ ☐ _____ = _____

2. Solve the story problems.

There are **4** 🐢 in the pond.
Then **3** more 🐢 come.

How many 🐢 are there in all?

_____ ☐ _____ = _____

There are **5** 🐕 under the tree.
1 more 🐕 comes.

How many 🐕 are there in total?

_____ ☐ _____ = _____

There are **2** 🐭 eating cheese.
2 more 🐭 come.

How many 🐭 are there altogether?

_____ ☐ _____ = _____

Subtracting from 0 to 5

1. Subtract. Use the key to colour the pictures.

Colour Key

0 – green
1 – blue
2 – red
3 – purple
4 – orange
5 – yellow

4 – 3 = _____   3 – 1 = _____   5 – 4 = _____

2 – 2 = _____   2 – 0 = _____   3 – 3 = _____

3 – 2 = _____   1 – 1 = _____   4 – 0 = _____

5 – 1 = _____   1 – 0 = _____   4 – 4 = _____

4 – 2 = _____   2 – 1 = _____   4 – 1 = _____

5 – 2 = _____   5 – 5 = _____   3 – 0 = _____

Subtracting from 0 to 5 (continued)

2. Subtract.

4	5	3
− 1	− 2	− 3

3	5	1	2	5
− 2	− 0	− 1	− 0	− 3

5	4	4	2	4
− 4	− 0	− 2	− 1	− 3

5	4	1	3	5
− 1	− 4	− 0	− 1	− 5

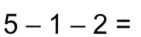

5 − 1 − 2 =   4 − 1 − 2 =

Subtracting from 0 to 10

1. Subtract. Use the key to colour the picture.

Colour Key
1 – red
2 – blue
3 – green
4 – orange
5 – brown
6 – yellow
7 – purple
8 – grey
9 – pink
10 – black

5 – 2 = _____

4 – 2 = _____

6 – 4 = _____

6 – 0 = _____

7 – 5 = _____

7 – 4 = _____

9 – 6 = _____

6 – 1 = _____

4 – 3 = _____

9 – 5 = _____

5 – 4 = _____

7 – 6 = _____

1 – 0 = _____

3 – 2 = _____

6 – 3 = _____

3 – 1 = _____

5 – 5 = _____

2 – 1 = _____

Subtracting from 0 to 10 (continued)

2. Subtract.

$$6 - 2 =$$ $$8 - 6 =$$ $$10 - 5 =$$

$$10 - 2 =$$ $$9 - 2 =$$ $$3 - 3 =$$ $$10 - 9 =$$ $$3 - 0 =$$

$$7 - 1 =$$ $$8 - 4 =$$ $$9 - 3 =$$ $$6 - 5 =$$ $$10 - 7 =$$

$$4 - 4 =$$ $$6 - 2 =$$ $$7 - 2 =$$ $$4 - 1 =$$ $$5 - 1 =$$

BRAIN STRETCH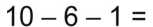

$$10 - 6 - 1 =$$ $$10 - 5 - 2 =$$

3. Subtract.

5	9	6
− 0	− 7	− 6

10	8	10	10	4
− 4	− 2	− 3	− 8	− 0

6	10	8	2	7
− 3	− 1	− 5	− 0	− 3

10	5	9	8	7
− 6	− 3	− 8	− 3	− 7

Subtracting from 0 to 20

1. Subtract. Use the number line to count back.

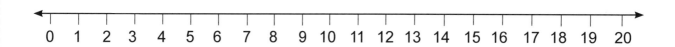

9	14	12	11	13
− 4	− 2	− 8	− 5	− 2

10	13	11	15	20
− 0	− 1	− 6	− 2	− 3

18	16	11	16	12
− 9	− 2	− 4	− 8	− 9

18	14	12	20	15
− 8	− 7	− 6	− 10	− 4

Story Problems

1. Solve the story problems.

There are **8**  on the ground.
Then **3** go away.

How many are left?

_____ ☐ _____ = _____

There are **7** on the flower.
Then **4** fly away.

How many are left?

_____ ☐ _____ = _____

There are **9** on the branch.
Then **3** fly away.

How many are left?

_____ ☐ _____ = _____

2. Solve the story problems.

There are **6**  in the pond.
Then **2** swim away.

How many are left?

_____ [ ] _____ = _____

There are **3** under the tree.
Then **1** runs away.

How many are left?

_____ [ ] _____ = _____

There are **5** eating cheese.
Then **4** go away.

How many are left?

_____ [ ] _____ = _____

Subtraction Sentence Match

1. Match the subtraction sentence to the answer.

12 – 6 =	10
7 – 3 =	2
10 – 2 =	5
6 – 5 =	4
9 – 6 =	7
5 – 3 =	9
9 – 4 =	11
8 – 1 =	0
10 – 1 =	6
11 – 0 =	3
1 – 1 =	8
10 – 0 =	1

Equal Parts

1. Circle the shape that shows two equal parts. Each part is a half. Colour one half.

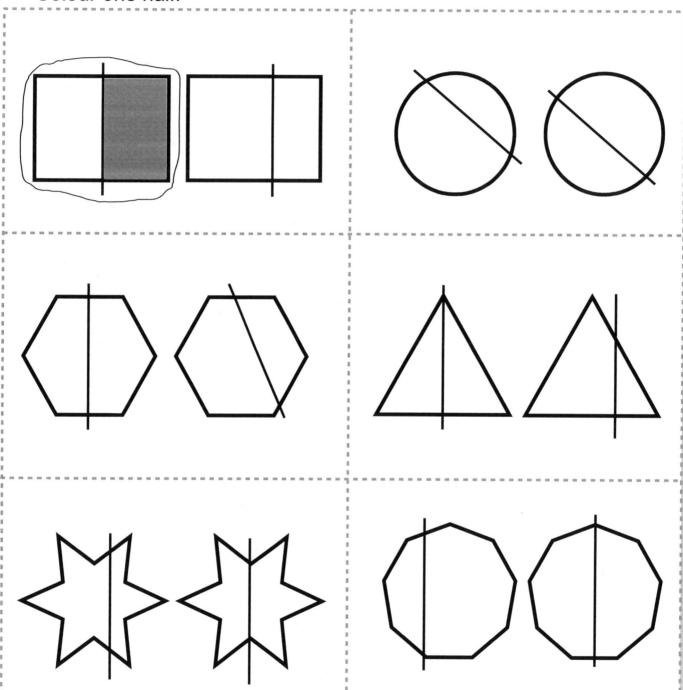

Colouring One Half

1. Colour one half of the set.

 $\dfrac{1}{2}$ means one part of 2 parts.

One half of the circles are coloured.

Colour $\dfrac{1}{2}$ green.

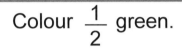

Colour $\dfrac{1}{2}$ red.

Colour $\dfrac{1}{2}$ blue.

Colour $\dfrac{1}{2}$ green.

Colour $\dfrac{1}{2}$ red.

Colour $\dfrac{1}{2}$ blue.

Naming the Fraction

1. What part is shaded? Circle the fraction.

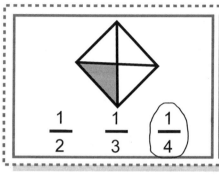

$\frac{1}{2}$ $\frac{1}{3}$ $\boxed{\frac{1}{4}}$

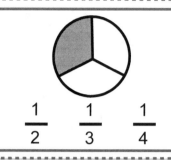

$\frac{1}{2}$ $\frac{1}{3}$ $\frac{1}{4}$

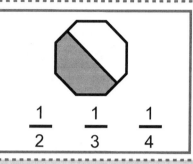

$\frac{1}{2}$ $\frac{1}{3}$ $\frac{1}{4}$

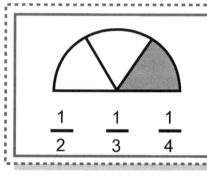

$\frac{1}{2}$ $\frac{1}{3}$ $\frac{1}{4}$

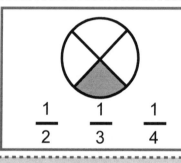

$\frac{1}{2}$ $\frac{1}{3}$ $\frac{1}{4}$

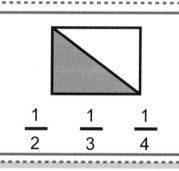

$\frac{1}{2}$ $\frac{1}{3}$ $\frac{1}{4}$

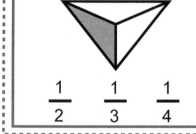

$\frac{1}{2}$ $\frac{1}{3}$ $\frac{1}{4}$

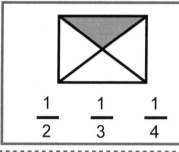

$\frac{1}{2}$ $\frac{1}{3}$ $\frac{1}{4}$

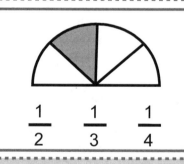

$\frac{1}{2}$ $\frac{1}{3}$ $\frac{1}{4}$

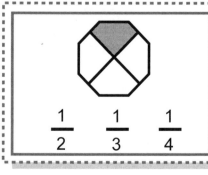

$\frac{1}{2}$ $\frac{1}{3}$ $\frac{1}{4}$

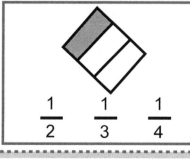

$\frac{1}{2}$ $\frac{1}{3}$ $\frac{1}{4}$

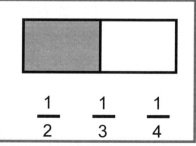

$\frac{1}{2}$ $\frac{1}{3}$ $\frac{1}{4}$

Repeating Patterns

A pattern repeats. A pattern can be different shapes and sizes. The core of the pattern are the parts that repeat over and over.

1. Circle the core of each repeating pattern. Extend the pattern.

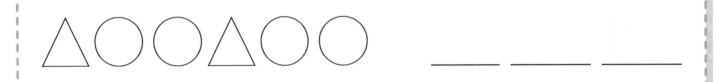

Repeating Patterns (continued)

2. Circle the core of each repeating pattern. Extend the pattern.

 _____ _____ _____

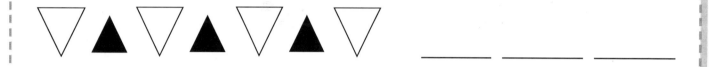 _____ _____ _____

 _____ _____ _____

 _____ _____ _____

 _____ _____ _____

 _____ _____ _____

Using Letters to Name Patterns

1. Use a letter to name each part of the pattern. Circle the core of the pattern.

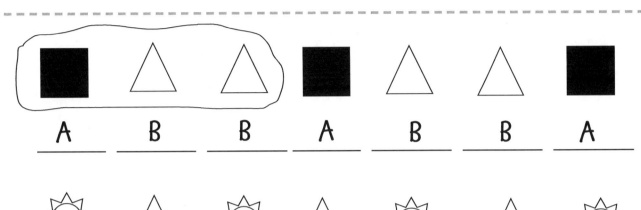

A   B   B   A   B   B   A

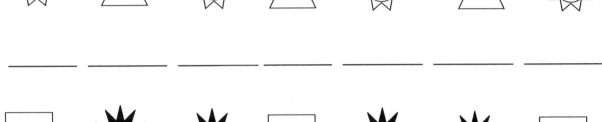

_____ _____ _____ _____ _____ _____ _____

_____ _____ _____ _____ _____ _____ _____

Draw your own pattern. Use a letter to name each part of the pattern.

_____ _____ _____ _____ _____ _____ _____

Draw your own pattern. Use a letter to name each part of the pattern.

_____ _____ _____ _____ _____ _____ _____

Creating Patterns

1. Create the pattern. Circle the core.

Colour an AB pattern.

Colour an ABC pattern.

Colour an AAB pattern.

Colour an ABBC pattern.

Make a pattern in which the size of the shape changes.

_____ _____ _____ _____ _____ _____

Make a pattern in which the position of the shape changes.

_____ _____ _____ _____ _____ _____

What Comes Next?

Make your own pattern. Use two or three colours.

1. Colour the ice-cream scoops. Then extend the pattern.

orange

red

brown

pink

green

blue

yellow

purple

red

2D Shapes

1. Complete.

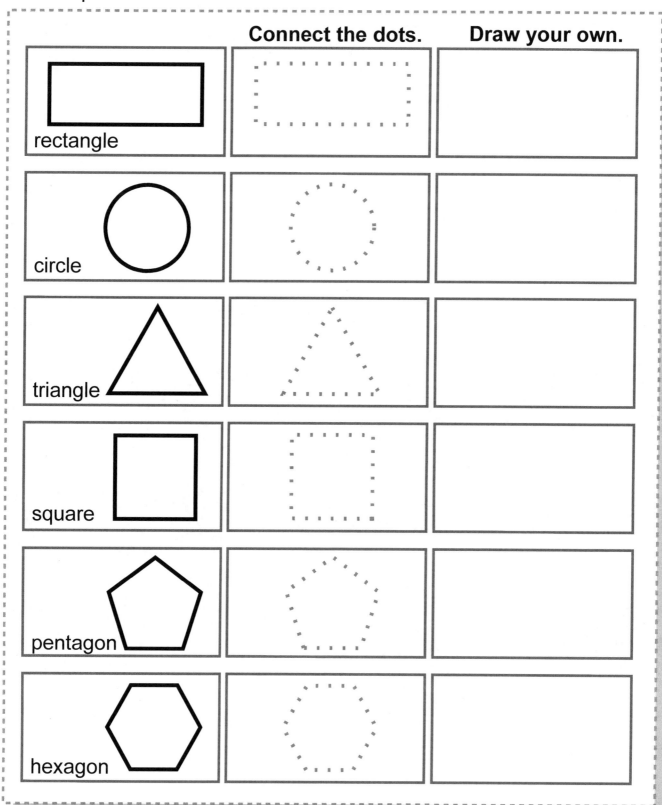

	Connect the dots.	Draw your own.
rectangle		
circle		
triangle		
square		
pentagon		
hexagon		

Matching 2D Shapes

1. Match the shape to its name.

square

pentagon

hexagon

triangle

circle

rectangle

What 2D Shapes Do You Know?

1. How many sides and corners does each shape have?

	Number of Sides	Number of Corners
rectangle		
circle		
triangle		
square		
rhombus		
pentagon		

Drawing Shapes

1. Use the shapes to draw a picture.

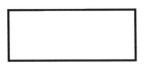

rectangle

circle

triangle

square

Sorting 2D Shapes

1. Read the sorting rule. Colour the shapes that follow the rule.

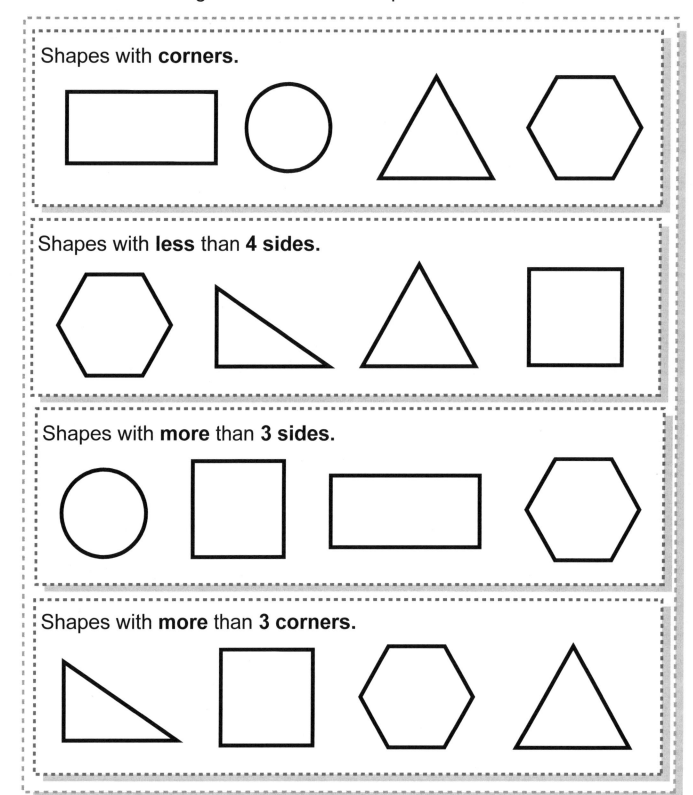

Shapes with **corners.**

Shapes with **less** than **4 sides.**

Shapes with **more** than **3 sides.**

Shapes with **more** than **3 corners.**

Symmetry

A **line of symmetry** divides a shape into 2 parts that are the exact same size and shape. Some shapes have 2 lines of symmetry.

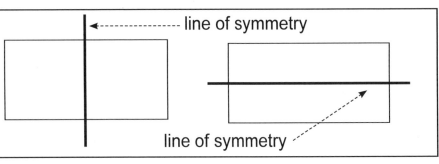

1. Draw a line of symmetry to show two sides exactly the same.

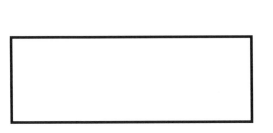

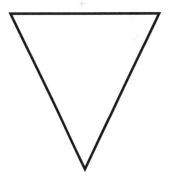

Symmetrical Shape

1. Draw the other half of each shape.

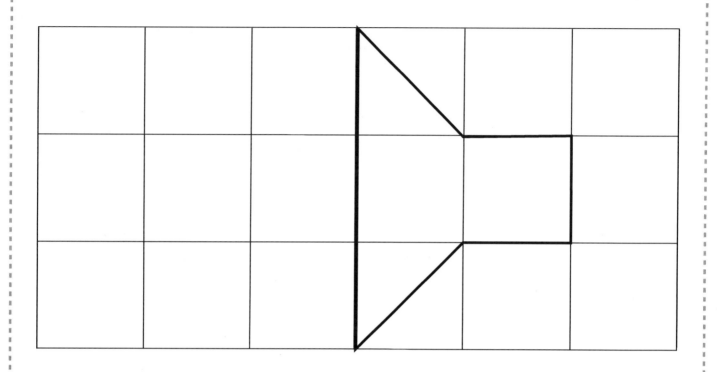

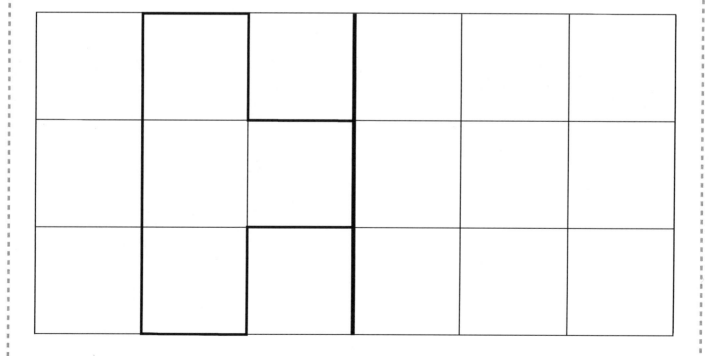

Symmetrical Shape

Matching 3D Objects

1. Match the 3D object to the image it looks like.

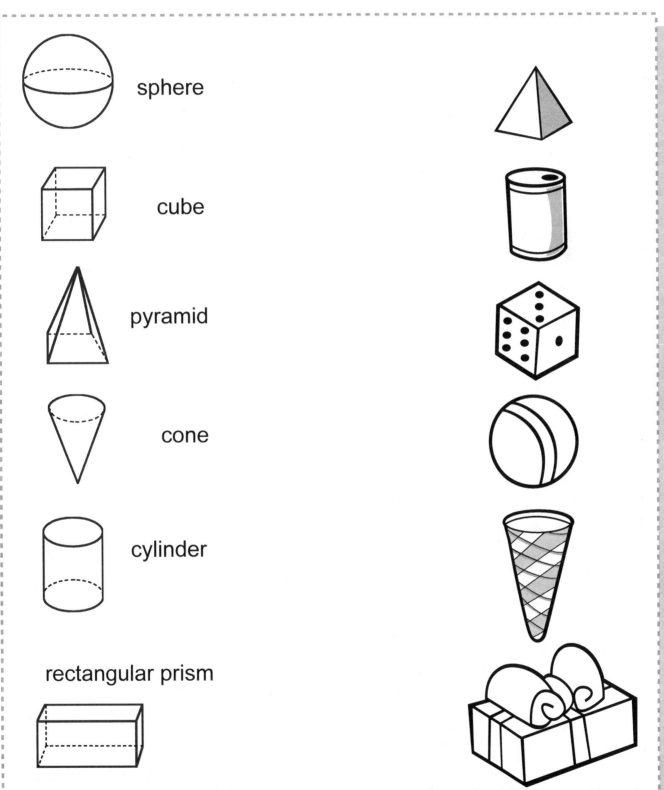

sphere

cube

pyramid

cone

cylinder

rectangular prism

Sorting 3D Objects

1. Read the rule. Circle the objects that follow the rule.

Circle the objects that **can** roll.

    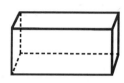

Circle the objects that **cannot** roll.

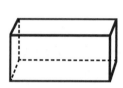  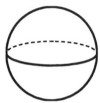 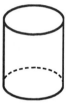

Circle the objects that you **can** stack on each other.

  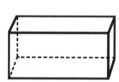  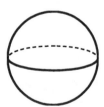

Circle the objects that you **cannot** stack on each other.

 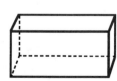  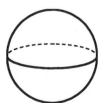

Following Directions

1. Read the directions and colour the picture.

Colour the bird on **top** of the apples black.
Colour the sun **above** the tree yellow.
Colour the apples **under** the bird red.
Colour the dog **next to** the tree brown.
Colour the apples on the **left** of the tree green.
Colour the grass **below** the tree green.

The Hour Hand

A clock has an hour hand.
The hour hand is short. It shows the hour.

You can write the time in two ways.
It is **5 o'clock** or **5:00**.

1. Draw a line between the times that are the same.

7 o'clock	1:00
6:00	7:00
1 o'clock	12 o'clock
12:00	6 o'clock

2. Write the time in two ways.

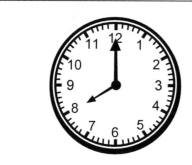

_____ o'clock or _____:00

_____ o'clock or _____:00

_____ o'clock or _____:00

_____ o'clock or _____:00

The Minute Hand

A clock has an hour hand. The hour hand is short. It shows the hour.

It is **3 o'clock** or **3:00**. There are 60 minutes in an hour.

A clock has a minute hand. The minute hand is long. It shows the minutes after the hour.

Count by 5s. It is 30 minutes after 3 o'clock. It is **half past 3** or **3:30**.

1. What time is it? Write the time two ways.

1. _____   2. _____

1. _____   2. _____

1. _____   2. _____

1. _____   2. _____

Telling Time to the Hour

1. Tell the time to the hour. Highlight the hour hand blue.
   Highlight the minute hand red. Hint: The minute hand is long.

_____ o'clock   _____ o'clock   _____ o'clock

_____ o'clock   _____ o'clock   _____ o'clock

_____ o'clock   _____ o'clock   _____ o'clock

_____ o'clock   _____ o'clock   _____ o'clock

Showing the Time to the Hour

1. Draw the two hands on the clock to show the time.
   Highlight the hour hand blue. Highlight the minute hand red.

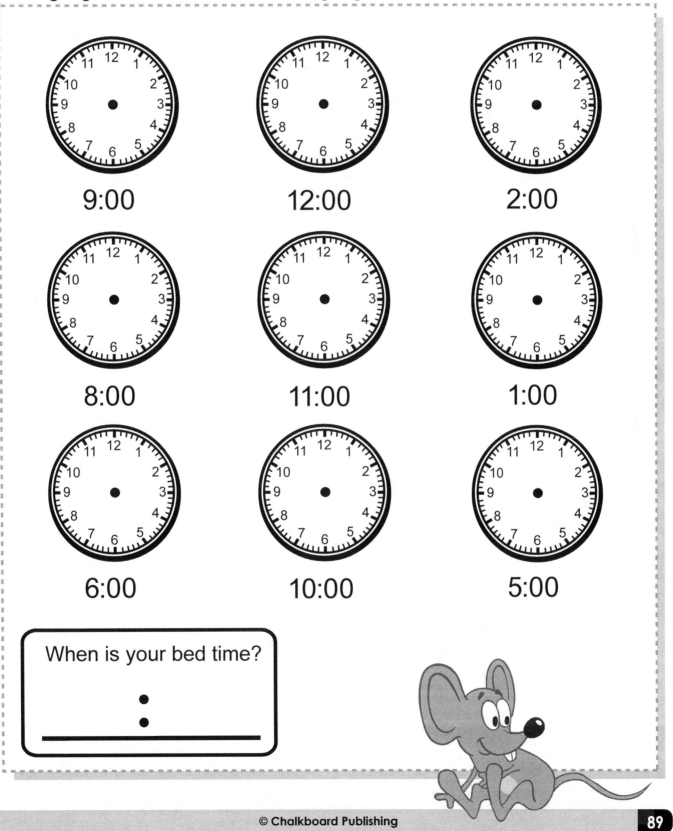

9:00

12:00

2:00

8:00

11:00

1:00

6:00

10:00

5:00

When is your bed time?

:

Telling Time to the Half Hour

1. Tell the time to the half hour.
   Highlight the hour hand blue. Highlight the minute hand red.

half past _____

half past _____

half past _____

half past _____

half past _____

half past _____

half past _____

half past _____

half past _____

half past _____

half past _____

half past _____

What Time Is It?

1. Circle the correct time.
   Highlight the hour hand blue. Highlight the minute hand red.

4:00 or 4:30

10:00 or 10:30

3:00 or 3:30

11:00 or 11:30

3:00 or 3:30

8:00 or 8:30

7:00 or 7:30

5:00 or 5:30

12:00 or 12:30

2:00 or 2:30

4:00 or 4:30

9:00 or 9:30

Time Match

1. Match the clock to the time.
   Highlight the hour hand blue. Highlight the minute hand red.

2:00

7:30

4:00

11:00

Canadian Coins

Each Canadian coin has a value.

This is a nickel.  5¢   5 cents

¢ means cents

This is a dime. 10¢   10 cents

This is a quarter.  25¢   25 cents

This is a loonie.  100¢   100 cents or 1 dollar

This is a toonie.  200¢   200 cents or 2 dollars

Getting to Know Coins

1. Draw a line from the coin to its value.
   Then match the coin to its name.

100 cents   toonie

25 cents   loonie

5 cents   nickel

200 cents   dime

10 cents   quarter

Getting to Know Coins (continued)

2. ▶ Circle the loonies red.   ▶ Circle the quarters green.
    ▶ Circle the dimes blue.   ▶ Circle the nickels yellow.
    ▶ Circle the toonies orange.

BRAIN STRETCH

How many loonies? _____   How many nickels? _____

How many dimes? _____   How many quarters? _____

How many toonies? _____

Adding Coins

1. Write how much money in total.

 = _____ ¢

_____ + _____ + _____ + _____ = _____ cents

_____ + _____ = _____ ¢

_____ + _____ + _____ = _____ cents

_____ + _____ = _____ ¢

Subtracting Coins

1. Write how much money is left.

 – = _____ cents

  – = _____ ¢

   – = _____ cents

  –   = _____ ¢

BRAIN STRETCH

Draw coins to help solve the problem.

Ahmed has 2 nickels. He finds 1 more. How much money does he have in total?

_____ ¢

Remi has 3 nickels. She loses 1 nickel. How much money does she have left?

_____ ¢

Counting Nickels

1. Count by 5s to find the value of the nickels.

_____ ¢ _____ ¢ _____ ¢ = _____ ¢

_____ ¢ _____ ¢ _____ ¢ _____ ¢ _____ ¢ _____ ¢ = _____ ¢

_____ ¢ _____ ¢ _____ ¢ _____ ¢ _____ ¢ = _____ ¢

_____ ¢ _____ ¢ _____ ¢ _____ ¢ = _____ ¢

_____ ¢ _____ ¢ _____ ¢ _____ ¢ _____ ¢ _____ ¢ _____ ¢ = _____ ¢

Counting Dimes

1. Count by 10s to find the value of the dimes.

_____ ¢ _____ ¢ _____ ¢ _____ ¢ = _____ ¢

_____ ¢ _____ ¢ _____ ¢ _____ ¢ _____ ¢ _____ ¢ = _____ ¢

_____ ¢ _____ ¢ = _____ ¢

_____ ¢ _____ ¢ _____ ¢ _____ ¢ _____ ¢ _____ ¢ _____ ¢ = _____ ¢

BRAIN STRETCH

One dime is equal to _____ nickels.
Draw a picture to show how you know.

Candy Counter

1. How much does each candy cost?

    ¢

    ¢

  ¢

     ¢

  ¢

Exploring Tally Charts

A tally chart counts data in 1s and groups of 5.

Each single tally mark stands for 1 vote. |

Each group of five tally marks stands for 5 votes.

Ms. Yen's class made a tally chart of their favourite ice cream.
Count the tally marks.

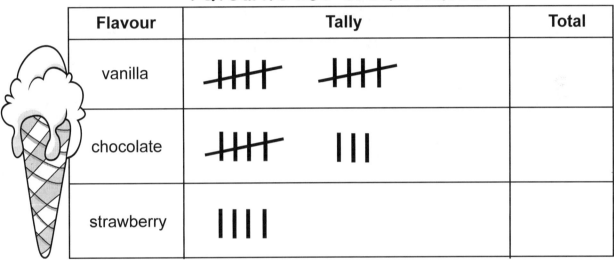

Favourite Ice Cream Flavour

Flavour	Tally	Total
vanilla	ⅢⅢ ⅢⅢ	
chocolate	ⅢⅢ |||	
strawberry	||||	

1. How many children picked vanilla? _____

2. How many children picked chocolate? _____

3. How many children picked strawberry? _____

4. Which ice cream was **most** popular? _____

5. Which ice cream was **least** popular? _____

Exploring Tally Charts

Here are the results of a favourite colour survey. Complete the tally chart.

My Favourite Colour Survey

Colour	Tally	Total
red	~~||||~~ ||	
blue	~~||||~~ ||||	
green	||||	
purple	~~||||~~		

1. What was the **most** popular colour? _____

2. What was the **least** popular colour? _____

3. What colour had 7 votes? _____

4. How many votes were there for red and blue altogether?

   _____

5. List the colours from the **most** votes to the **least** votes.

_____

Exploring Pictographs

A pictograph uses pictures to show information or data.

Mrs. Turnbull's class made a pictograph of their favourite pet fish survey.

Each 👤 equals 1 vote. Count the number of 👤 in each row.

Fish	Number of Children Who Liked Each Fish
🐟	👤 👤 👤 👤
🐟	👤 👤 👤 👤 👤 👤 👤 👤 👤 👤
🐟	👤 👤 👤 👤 👤 👤 👤

1. How many children chose  ? _____

2. How many children chose  ? _____

3. How many children chose  ? _____

4. Circle the **most** popular fish. Mark with an X the **least** popular fish.

Exploring Pictographs

Mr. Shaw's class made a favourite animal pictograph.

Each ☿ equals 1 vote. Count the number of ☿ in each row.

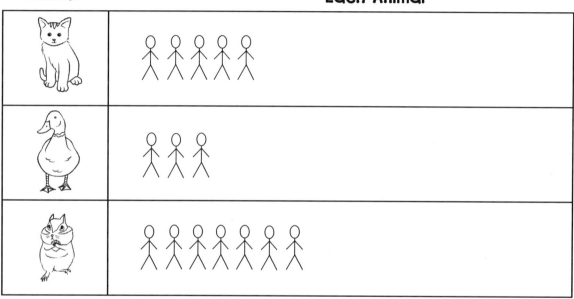

Animal	Number of Children Who Liked Each Animal

1. How many children chose ? _____

2. How many children chose ? _____

3. How many children chose ? _____

4. Circle the **most** popular animal.

   Mark with an X the **least**

   popular animal.

Exploring Bar Graphs

A bar graph uses bars to show data.
This bar graph shows the favourite winter activity of children.

Read the bar graph to answer the questions.

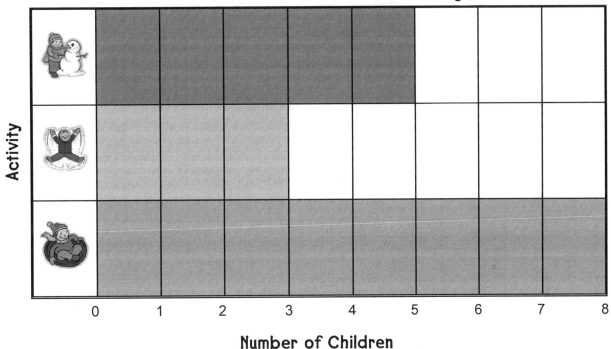

Favourite Winter Activity

Activity

Number of Children

1. How many votes? _____  _____ _____

2. Circle the **most** popular winter activity.

3. Circle the **least** popular winter activity.

Exploring Bar Graphs

Ms. Stanley's class took a survey of their favourite pets.
Count the votes for each pet and complete the bar graph.

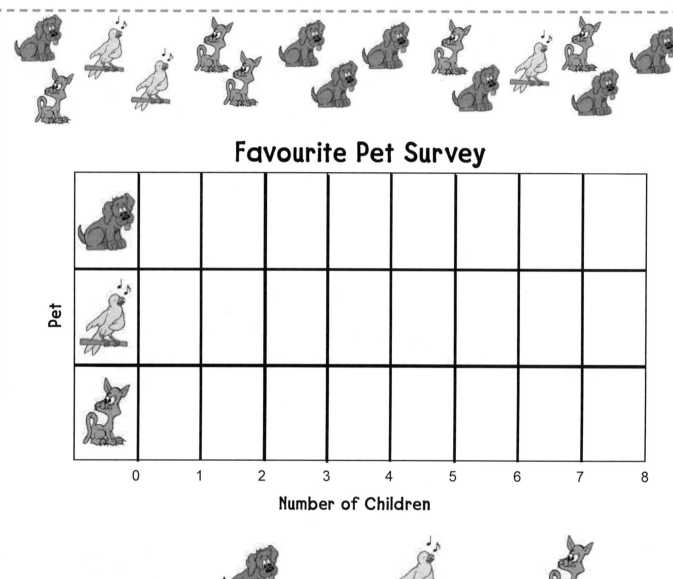

Favourite Pet Survey

Pet

0   1   2   3   4   5   6   7   8

Number of Children

1. How many votes?   _____   _____   _____

2. Circle the pet that 3 children chose as their favourite pet.

Exploring Graphs

Here are the results of a favourite treat survey. Complete the tally chart.

Treats We Like

Treat	Tally	Total
🧅	IIII	
🍦	IIIII	
🍬	II	

Use the information from the tally chart to make a bar graph.
1 tally = 1 coloured box.

Treats We Like

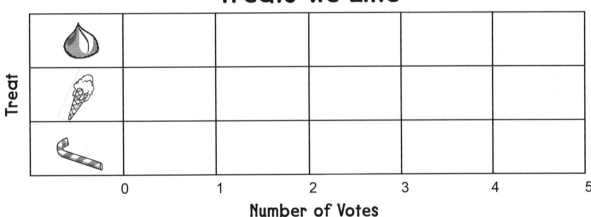

Treat

0   1   2   3   4   5

Number of Votes

Answer the questions.

1. Circle the **most** popular treat.

2. Put an X on the **least** popular treat.

Comparing Height

1. Number the animals in order from the tallest to shortest. Use 1, 2, and 3.

© Chalkboard Publishing

Exploring Measuring with Non-standard Units

1. Count the stars to measure the length of the spaceships.
   About how long is each spaceship?

★

★

★

★

Exploring Centimetres

1. How many centimetres long is each pencil?

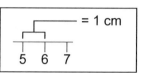

= 1 cm

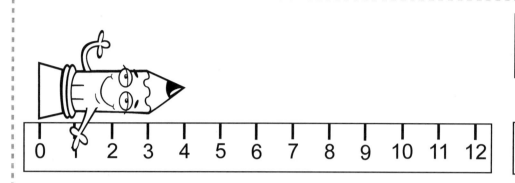

| centimetres |

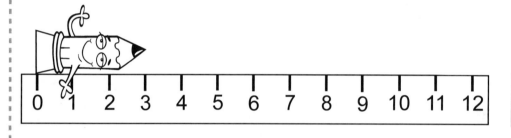

| centimetres |

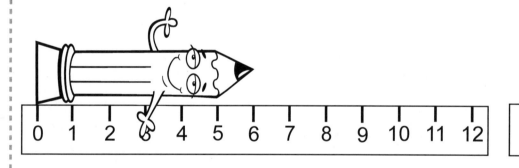

| centimetres |

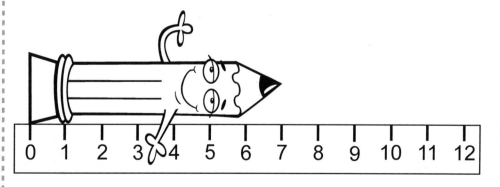

| centimetres |

Exploring Mass

Mass measures how much something weighs.

1. What is the mass of the creature? Count the blocks to find out.

_____ blocks

_____ blocks

_____ blocks

_____ blocks

Exploring Mass (continued)

2. Some blocks are missing. Draw blocks to make the same mass on both sides.

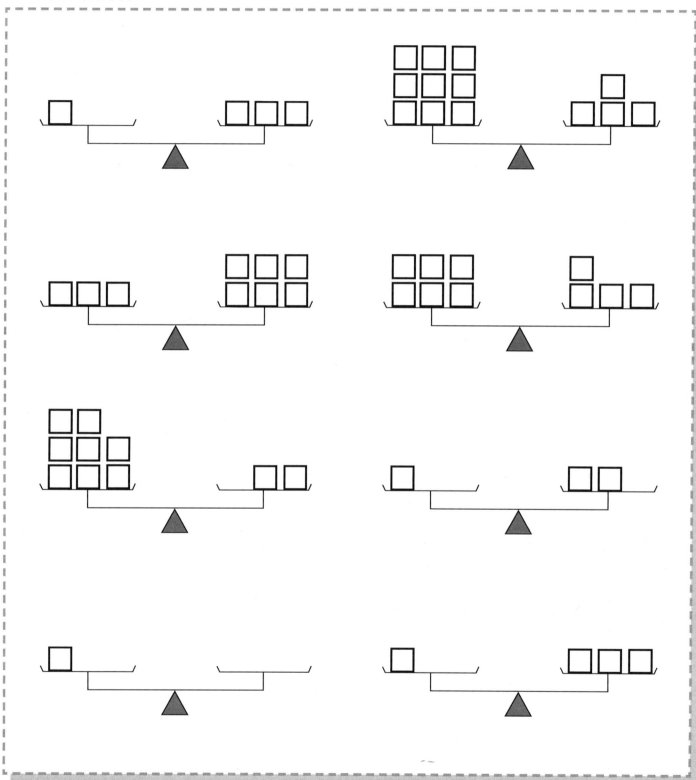

Fantastic Work!

You are
a math
expert!

Number Words pp. 1–2

1. Students trace the numerals and number words from 1 to 5. They draw a line from each of 1 to 5 to the correct number of counters. **2.** Students trace the numerals and number words from 6 to 10. They draw a line from each of 6 to 10 to the correct number of counters.

Numbers p. 3

1. Students trace the numerals and draw dots for each: 9, 9 dots; 4, 4 dots; 7, 7 dots; 8, 8 dots; 2, 2 dots; 5, 5 dots; 10, 10 dots

Counting to 10 Using Ten-Frames p. 4

1. 9 counters; 6 counters; 5 counters; 8 counters; 1 counter; 2 counters; 7 counters; 10 counters; 3 counters; 4 counters

Comparing Numbers from 1 to 10 p. 5

1. 4 is <u>less than</u> 6; 10 is <u>greater than</u> 5; 7 is <u>greater than</u> 2; 4 is <u>equal to</u> 4; 8 is <u>less than</u> 9; 3 is <u>greater than</u> 1

Numbers and Number Words p. 6

A line drawn from the numeral to the number word: 2, two, 3, three, 4, four; 5, five; 6, six; 7, seven; 8, eight; 9, nine; 10, ten; Brain Stretch: Students circle "four."

Number Word Search p. 7

s	z	e	r	o	o	n	e
e	t	t	f	n	i	n	e
v	w	e	o	f	h	o	s
e	o	n	u	q	t	b	i
n	k	z	r	e	k	l	x
a	b	e	i	g	h	t	v
s	t	h	r	e	e	n	x
t	p	w	f	i	v	e	v

Count and Write the Number p. 8

1. (6) (7) (7) (8)(4)

More, Fewer, and Less pp. 9–10

2. A circle around the set of 4; <u>4</u> is <u>more</u> than <u>3</u>. **3.** A circle around the set of 3; <u>3</u> is <u>less</u> than <u>5</u>. **4.** A circle around the set of 8; <u>8</u> is <u>more</u> than <u>6</u>. **5.** A drawing of 6 circles; a drawing of 4 squares; a drawing of 4 triangles; a drawing of 3 circles

Using Ten-Frames to Count to 20 pp. 11–14

1. 17 counters; 15 counters; 11 counters; 18 counters; 20 counters; 16 counters; 14 counters; 12 counters; 19 counters
2. First ten-frame is full, second ten-frame has 5 counters; First ten-frame is full, second ten-frame has 1 counter; First ten-frame is full, second ten-frame has 7 counters; First ten-frame is full, second ten-frame has 2 counters **3.** Both ten-frames are full; First ten-frame is full, second ten-frame has 4 counters; First ten-frame is full; second ten-frame has 9 counters; First ten-frame is full, second ten-frame has 1 counter **4.** First ten-frame is full, second ten-frame has 6 counters; First ten-frame is full, second ten-frame has 8 counters; First ten-frame is full, second ten-frame has 3 counters; First ten-frame is full, second ten-frame has 0 counters

Counting from 0 to 20 p. 15

1. Students connect the dots from 0 to 20.

Ordering Numbers p. 16

1. <u>3</u>, 4, 5; 13, 14, <u>15</u>; <u>15</u>, 16, <u>17</u>; 5, <u>6</u>, 7; 16, 17, <u>18</u>; 12, <u>13</u>, 14; <u>7</u>, 8, <u>9</u>; 15, 16, <u>17</u>; <u>16</u>, 17, 18; Brain Stretch: Students circle "17."

Counting to 50 p. 17

1. Students connect the dots from 0 to 50.

Counting to 100 p. 18

7, 15, 19, 21, 24, 27, 30, 31, 42, 44, 46, 49, 53, 55, 58, 60, 62, 63, 65, 67, 76, 78, 84, 86, 91, 98, 99

Counting by 2s to 100 p. 19

Students connect the dots by counting by 2s to 100. Answers will vary. Example: Worm; Brain Stretch: 4, 6, 8, 10

Counting by 5s to 100 p. 20

Students connect the dots by counting by 5s to 100. Answers will vary. Example: Dragon Man; Brain Stretch: 10, 15, 20, 25

Ordinal Numbers to 10 p. 21

1. seco<u>nd</u>, 2nd; thi<u>rd</u>, 3<u>rd</u>; four<u>th</u>, 4<u>th</u>; fif<u>th</u>, 5<u>th</u>; six<u>th</u>, 6<u>th</u>; seven<u>th</u>, 7<u>th</u>; eigh<u>th</u>, 8<u>th</u>; nin<u>th</u>, 9<u>th</u>; ten<u>th</u>, 10<u>th</u>

2. a) 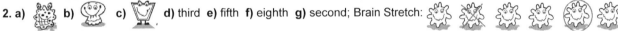 **b)** **c)** **d)** third **e)** fifth **f)** eighth **g)** second; Brain Stretch:

Groups of 10 pp. 22–23

2. 2; 3; 23 **3.** 1; 6; 16 **4.** 1; 3; 13 **5.** 2; 4; 24 **6.** 1; 9; 19

Tens and Ones pp. 24–25

1. <u>2</u> tens + <u>8</u> ones = <u>28</u> ones **2.** <u>1</u> ten + <u>5</u> ones = <u>15</u> ones **3.** <u>3</u> tens + <u>3</u> ones = <u>33</u> ones **4.** <u>4</u> tens + <u>7</u> ones = <u>47</u> ones

5. <u>5</u> tens + <u>0</u> ones = <u>50</u> ones **6.** <u>2</u> tens + <u>1</u> one = <u>21</u> ones **7.** <u>9</u> tens + <u>4</u> ones = <u>94</u> ones **8.** <u>3</u> tens + <u>5</u> ones = <u>35</u> ones

9. <u>2</u> tens + <u>4</u> ones = <u>24</u> ones **10.** <u>4</u> tens + <u>5</u> ones = <u>45</u> ones **11.** <u>6</u> tens + <u>0</u> ones = <u>60</u> ones **12.** <u>1</u> ten + <u>8</u> ones = <u>18</u> ones;

Brain Stretch: A drawing of 2 tens and 3 ones; 23

Addition Stories pp. 26–28

1. 3 + 3 = 6 **2.** 3 + 4 = 7 **3.** 1 + 10 = 11 **4.** 2 + 3 = 5 **5.** 5 + 5 = 10 **6.** 7 + 4 = 11 **7.** 4 + 1 = 5 **8.** 5 + 6 = 11 **9.** 1 + 5 = 6

10. 8 + 4 = 12 **11.** 7 + 3 = 10 **12.** 2 + 4 = 6 **13.** 8 + 1 = 9 **14.** 6 + 3 = 9 **15.** 3 + 6 = 9 **16.** 6 + 4 = 10 **17.** 4 + 2 = 6

18. 5 + 1 = 6 **19.** 4 + 5 = 9 **20.** 4 + 4 = 8 **21.** 9 + 2 = 11 **22.** 1 + 7 = 8 **23.** 3 + 8 = 11 **24.** 7 + 5= 12

Adding 1 or 2 by Counting On pp. 29–30

1. 4; 3, <u>4</u>; 9, 7, <u>8</u>, <u>9</u>; 6, 5, <u>6</u>; 3, 1, <u>2</u>, <u>3</u>; 17, 16, <u>17</u>; 20, 18, <u>19</u>, <u>20</u>

2. 10, 9, <u>10</u>; 5, 3, <u>4</u>, <u>5</u>; 7, 6, <u>7</u>; 16, 14, <u>15</u>, <u>16</u>; 2, 1, <u>2</u>; 10, 8, <u>9</u>, <u>10</u>; 8, 7, <u>8</u>; 7, 5, <u>6</u>, <u>7</u>; 9, 8, <u>9</u>; 2, 0,<u>1</u>, <u>2</u>, 18, 17, <u>18</u>; 15, 13, <u>14</u>, <u>15</u>;

Addition Doubles p. 31

1 + 1 = 2 **2.** 2 + 2 = 4 **3.** 3 + 3 = 6 **4.** 4 + 4 = 8 **5.** 5 + 5 = 10 **6.** 6 + 6 = 12

Using a Number Line to Add pp. 32–33

Note: Students may show the dot at either addend (commutative property).

1. 2 + 6 = <u>8</u>, a number line showing a dot at 2 and 6 jumps from 2 to 8; 6 + 4 = <u>10</u>, a number line showing a dot at 6 and 4 jumps from 6 to 10; 1 + 8 = <u>9</u>, a number line showing a dot at 1 and 8 jumps from 1 to 9; 2 + 7 = <u>9</u>, a number line showing a dot at 2 and 7 jumps from 2 to 9.

2. 0 + 5 = <u>5</u>, a number line showing a dot at 0 and 5 jumps from 0 to 5; 7 + 2 = <u>9</u>, a number line showing a dot at 7 and 2 jumps from 7 to 9; 5 + 1 = <u>6</u>, a number line showing a dot at 5 and 1 jump from 5 to 6; 2 + 3 = <u>5</u>, a number line showing a dot at 2 and 3 jumps from 2 to 5; 4 + 4 = <u>8</u>, a number line showing a dot at 4 and 4 jumps from 4 to 8; 3 + 5 = <u>8</u>, a number line showing a dot at 3 and 5 jumps from 3 to 8; 5 + 4 = <u>9</u>, a number line showing a dot at 5 and 4 jumps from 5 to 9

Numbers Can Be Added in any Order pp. 34–35

1. 6 + 3 = <u>9</u>, 3 + 6 = <u>9</u>, one 10-frame shows 6 + 3 and the other one shows 3 + 6; 2 + 4 = <u>6</u>, 4 + 2 = <u>6</u>, one 10-frame shows 2 + 4 and the other one shows 4 + 2; 1 + 7 = <u>8</u>, 7 + 1 = <u>8</u>, one 10-frame shows 1 + 7 and the other one shows 7 + 1; 4 + 5 = <u>9</u>,

5 + 4 = <u>9</u>, one 10-frame shows 4 + 5 and the other one shows 5 + 4; 8 + 2 = <u>10</u>, 2 + 8 = <u>10</u>, one 10-frame shows 8 + 2 and the other one shows 2 + 8 **2.** 6 + 4 = <u>10</u>, 4 + 6 = <u>10</u>, one 10-frame shows 6 + 4 and the other one shows 4 + 6; 7 + 2 = <u>9</u>, 2 + 7 = <u>9</u>, one 10-frame shows 7 + 2 and the other one shows 2 + 7; 3 + 4 = <u>7</u>, 4 + 3 = <u>7</u>, one 10-frame shows 4 + 3 and the other one shows 3 + 4; 1 + 9 = <u>10</u>, 9 + 1 = <u>10</u>, one 10-frame shows 1 + 9 and the other one shows 9 + 1; 1 + 2 = <u>3</u>, 2 + 1 = <u>3</u>, one 10-frame shows 1 + 2 and the other one shows 2 + 1; Sample question: 0 + 2 = <u>2</u>, 2 + 0= <u>2</u>, one 10-frame shows 0 + 2 and the other one shows 2 + 0

Making 10 to Add p. 36

For each question, there should be a group of 10 circled.

5 + 7 = 10 + <u>2</u> = <u>12</u>; 7 + 7 = 10 + <u>4</u> = <u>14</u>; 4 + 9 = 10 + <u>3</u> = <u>13</u>; 5 + 8 = 10 + 3 = <u>13</u>; 9 + 6 = 10 + 5 = <u>15</u>

Making Addition Sentences pp. 37–38

Look for 3 addition sentences and blocks coloured correctly to represent each sum. Examples:

1. 1 + 3 = 4, 2 + 2 = 4, 4 + 0 = 4; 2 + 5 = 7, 5 + 2 = 7, 3 + 4 = 7; 1 + 8 = 9, 2 + 7 = 9, 3 + 6 = 9; 10 + 1 = 11, 9 + 2 = 11, 3 + 8 = 11 **2.** 2 + 8 = 10, 3 + 7 = 10, 4 + 6 = 10; 1 + 5 = 6, 2 + 4 = 6, 3 + 3 = 6; 4 + 8 = 12, 5 + 7 = 12, 6 + 6 = 12; 2 + 6 = 8, 4 + 4 = 8, 5 + 3 = 8

Subtraction Stories pp. 39–41

2. 2 − 1 = 1 **3.** 5 − 3 = 2 **4.** 8 − 1 = 7 **5.** 8 − 4 = 4 **6.** 7 − 1 = 6 **7.** 6 − 2 = 4 **8.** 6 − 3 = 3 **9.** 10 − 2 = 8 **10.** 12 − 4 = 8 **11.** 4 − 1 = 3 **12.** 8 − 2 = 6 **13.** 8 − 7 = 1 **14.** 7 − 2 = 5 **15.** 6 − 1 = 5 **16.** 8 − 4 = 4 **17.** 10 − 5 = 5 **18.** 12 − 5 = 7 **19.** 4 − 2 = 2 **20.** 8 − 6 = 2 **21.** 11 − 3 = 8 **22.** 7 − 3 = 4 **23.** 6 − 2 = 4 **24.** 8 − 5 = 3

Subtracting 1 or 2 by Counting Back pp 42–43

1. 8; 9, <u>8</u>; 6, 8, <u>7</u>, <u>6</u>; 6, 7, <u>6</u>; 2, 4, <u>3</u>, <u>2</u>; 4, 5, <u>4</u>; 4, 6, <u>5</u>, <u>4</u>; 17, 18, <u>17</u>; 15, 17, <u>16</u>, <u>15</u> **2.** 3, 4, <u>3</u>; 7, 9, <u>8</u>, <u>7</u>; 1, 2, <u>1</u>; 8, 10, <u>9</u>, <u>8</u>; 5, 6, <u>5</u>; 5, 7, <u>6</u>, <u>5</u>; 7, 8, <u>7</u>; 10, 12, <u>11</u>, <u>10</u>; 12, 13, <u>12</u>; 1, 3, <u>2</u>, <u>1</u>; 14, 15, <u>14</u>; 9, 11, <u>10</u>, <u>9</u>; 11, 12, <u>11</u>; 17, 19, <u>18</u>, <u>17</u>

Using a Number Line to Subtract pp 44–45

1. 9 − 6 = <u>3</u>, a number line showing a dot at 9 and 6 jumps back from 9 to 3; 6 − 3 = <u>3</u>, a number line showing a dot at 6 and 3 jumps back from 6 to 3; 4 − 2 = <u>2</u>, a number line showing a dot at 4 and 2 jumps back from 4 to 2; 7 − 1 = <u>6</u>, a number line showing a dot at 7 and 1 jump back from 7 to 6. **2.** 9 − 5 = <u>4</u>, a number line showing a dot at 9 and 5 jumps back from 9 to 4; 5 − 3 = <u>2</u>, a number line showing a dot at 5 and 3 jumps back from 5 to 2; 7 − 2 = <u>5</u>, a number line showing a dot at 7 and 2 jumps back from 7 to 5; 8 − 1 = <u>7</u>, a number line showing a dot at 8 and 1 jump back from 8 to 7; 10 − 4 = <u>6</u>, a number line showing a dot at 10 and 4 jumps back from 10 to 6; 3 − 3 = <u>0</u>, a number line showing a dot at 3 and 3 jumps back from 3 to 0; 9 − 8 = <u>1</u>, a number line showing a dot at 9 and 8 jumps back from 9 to 1

Making Subtraction Sentences pp 46–47

1. Look for 3 subtraction sentences and blocks coloured correctly to represent each subtraction. Examples: 9 − 4 = 5 (4 blocks crossed out and 5 blocks coloured), 9 − 5 = 4 (5 blocks crossed out and 4 blocks coloured), 9 − 7 = 2 (7 blocks crossed out and 2 blocks coloured); 6 − 4 = 2 (4 blocks crossed out and 2 blocks coloured), 6 − 5 = 1 (5 blocks crossed out and 1 block coloured), 6 − 3 = 3 (3 blocks crossed out and 3 blocks coloured); 4 − 3 = 1 (3 blocks crossed out and 1 block coloured), 4 − 2 = 2 (2 blocks crossed out and 2 blocks coloured), 4 − 0 = 4 (0 blocks crossed out and 4 blocks coloured); 10 − 4 = 6 (4 blocks crossed out and 6 blocks coloured), 10 − 5 = 5 (5 blocks crossed out and 5 blocks coloured), 10 − 7 = 3 (7 blocks crossed out and 3 blocks coloured) **2.** 7 − 4 = 3 (4 blocks crossed out and 3 blocks coloured), 7 − 5 = 2 (5 blocks crossed out and 2 blocks coloured), 7 − 7 = 0 (7 blocks crossed out and 0 blocks coloured); 5 − 4 = 1 (4 blocks crossed out and 1 blocks coloured), 5 − 2 = 3 (2 blocks crossed out and 3 blocks coloured), 5 − 3 = 2 (3 blocks crossed out and 2 blocks coloured); 8 − 4 = 4 (4 blocks crossed out and 4 blocks coloured), 8 − 5 = 3 (5 blocks crossed out and 3 blocks coloured), 8 − 7 = 1 (7 blocks crossed out and 1 block coloured); 12 − 4 = 8 (4 blocks crossed out and 8 blocks coloured), 12 − 5 = 7 (5 blocks crossed out and 7 blocks coloured), 12 − 7 = 5 (7 blocks crossed out and 5 blocks coloured)

Sums to 5 pp. 48–49

1. Check that students colour the picture correctly. $4 + 1 = \underline{5}$; $3 + 1 = \underline{4}$; $1 + 1 = \underline{2}$; $2 + 0 = \underline{2}$; $5 + 0 = \underline{5}$; $2 + 3 = \underline{5}$; $1 + 3 = \underline{4}$; $0 + 1 = \underline{1}$; $0 + 5 = \underline{5}$; $2 + 2 = \underline{4}$; $1 + 4 = \underline{5}$; $2 + 1 = \underline{3}$; $1 + 0 = \underline{1}$; $3 + 2 = \underline{5}$; $4 + 0 = \underline{4}$; $0 + 4 = \underline{4}$; $0 + 0 = \underline{0}$; $0 + 2 = 2$ **2.** $4 + 1 = \underline{5}$; $2 + 2 = \underline{4}$; $0 + 2 = \underline{2}$; $5 + 0 = \underline{5}$; $0 + 4 = \underline{4}$; $0 + 3 = \underline{3}$; $3 + 2 = \underline{5}$; $1 + 3 = \underline{4}$; $3 + 0 = 3$; $4 + 0 = \underline{4}$; $1 + 4 = \underline{5}$; $2 + 3 = \underline{5}$; $1 + 1 = \underline{2}$; $0 + 1 = \underline{1}$; $2 + 1 = \underline{3}$; $3 + 1 = \underline{4}$; $1 + 0 = \underline{1}$; $1 + 2 = \underline{3}$

Sums to 10 pp. 50–54

1. Check that students colour the picture correctly. $2 + 1 = \underline{3}$; $1 + 2 = \underline{3}$; $3 + 6 = \underline{9}$; $5 + 2 = \underline{7}$; $6 + 0 = \underline{6}$; $0 + 3 = \underline{3}$; $3 + 4 = \underline{7}$; $1 + 1 = \underline{2}$; $1 + 0 = \underline{1}$; $2 + 2 = \underline{4}$; $1 + 5 = \underline{6}$; $4 + 4 = \underline{8}$; $3 + 1 = \underline{4}$; $2 + 3 = 5$; $4 + 1 = \underline{5}$; $2 + 5 = \underline{7}$; $6 + 1 = \underline{7}$; $3 + 7 = \underline{10}$ **2.** . $3 + 1 = \underline{4}$; $1 + 1 = \underline{2}$; $5 + 2 = \underline{7}$; $0 + 8 = \underline{8}$; $5 + 0 = \underline{5}$; $2 + 3 = \underline{5}$; $1 + 2 = \underline{3}$; $0 + 10 = \underline{10}$; $4 + 4 = \underline{8}$; $6 + 1 = \underline{7}$; $4 + 2 = \underline{6}$; $7 + 3 = \underline{10}$; $3 + 5 = \underline{8}$; $2 + 5 = \underline{7}$; $3 + 6 = \underline{9}$; $4 + 1 = \underline{5}$; $2 + 2 = \underline{4}$; $4 + 5 = \underline{9}$; Brain Stretch: 8; 10 **3.** $5 + 5 = \underline{10}$; $2 + 6 = \underline{8}$; $8 + 2 = \underline{10}$; $2 + 2 = \underline{4}$; $8 + 1 = \underline{9}$; $3 + 3 = \underline{6}$; $4 + 4 = \underline{8}$; $3 + 0 = \underline{3}$; $3 + 6 = \underline{9}$; $2 + 3 = \underline{5}$; $0 + 9 = \underline{9}$; $1 + 5 = \underline{6}$; $10 + 0 = \underline{10}$; $1 + 4 = \underline{5}$; $5 + 4 = \underline{9}$; $4 + 3 = \underline{7}$; $2 + 8 = \underline{10}$; $1 + 7 = \underline{8}$; Brain Stretch: $4 + 2 + 3 = \underline{9}$; $5 + 1 + 2 = \underline{8}$ **4.** $7 + 1 = \underline{8}$; $5 + 1 = \underline{6}$; $5 + 2 = \underline{7}$; $8 + 2 = \underline{10}$; $5 + 3 = \underline{8}$; $2 + 3 = \underline{5}$; $1 + 4 = \underline{5}$; $6 + 4 = \underline{10}$; $1 + 3 = \underline{4}$; $4 + 2 = \underline{6}$; $9 + 1 = \underline{10}$; $2 + 2 = \underline{4}$; $6 + 2 = \underline{8}$; $2 + 1 = \underline{3}$; $1 + 8 = \underline{9}$; $3 + 2 = \underline{5}$; $2 + 7 = \underline{9}$; $3 + 6 = 9$; Brain Stretch: $1 + 7 + 1 = \underline{9}$; $3 + 5 + 1 = \underline{9}$ **5.** $5 + 4 = \underline{9}$; $2 + 6 = \underline{8}$; $7 + 2 = \underline{9}$; $2 + 4 = \underline{6}$; $6 + 1 = \underline{7}$; $3 + 7 = \underline{10}$; $4 + 5 = 9$; $5 + 0 = \underline{5}$; $6 + 3 = \underline{9}$; $2 + 5 = \underline{7}$; $1 + 5 = \underline{6}$; $4 + 4 = \underline{8}$; $1 + 1 = \underline{2}$; $5 + 5 = \underline{10}$; $8 + 1 = \underline{9}$; $2 + 8 = \underline{10}$; $3 + 3 = \underline{6}$; $3 + 1 = \underline{4}$; Brain Stretch: $8 + 1 + 0 = \underline{9}$; $2 + 2 + 4 = \underline{8}$

Sums to 20 p. 55

1. $6 + 6 = \underline{12}$; $9 + 4 = \underline{13}$; $10 + 2 = \underline{12}$; $8 + 6 = \underline{14}$; $11 + 3 = \underline{14}$; $9 + 2 = \underline{11}$; $15 + 0 = \underline{15}$; $12 + 3 = \underline{15}$; $8 + 7 = \underline{15}$; $7 + 7 = \underline{14}$; $10 + 10 = \underline{20}$; $9 + 10 = \underline{19}$; $11 + 1 = \underline{12}$; $10 + 4 = \underline{14}$; $4 + 7 = \underline{11}$; $9 + 5 = \underline{14}$; $6 + 7 = \underline{13}$; $9 + 9 = \underline{18}$; $8 + 5 = \underline{13}$; $10 + 3 = \underline{13}$

Number Sentence Match p. 56

1. A line drawn from the number sentence to the answer: 3 + 5, 8; 1 + 0, 1; 2 + 2, 4; 4 + 2, 6; 5 + 5, 10; 2 + 1, 3; 8 + 3, 11; 6 + 6, 12; 7 + 2, 9; 5 + 2, 7; 1 + 1, 2; 3 + 2, 5

Story Problems pp. 57–58

1. $3 + 2 = 5$; $4 + 1 = 5$; $2 + 5 = 7$ **2.** $4 + 3 = 7$; $5 + 1 = 6$; $2 + 2 = 4$

Subtracting from 0 to 5 pp. 59–60

1. Check that students colour the picture correctly. $4 - 3 = \underline{1}$; $3 - 1 = \underline{2}$; $5 - 4 = \underline{1}$; $2 - 2 = \underline{0}$; $2 - 0 = \underline{2}$; $3 - 3 = \underline{0}$; $3 - 2 = \underline{1}$; $1 - 1 = \underline{0}$; $4 - 0 = \underline{4}$; $5 - 1 = \underline{4}$; $1 - 0 = \underline{1}$; $4 - 4 = \underline{0}$; $4 - 2 = \underline{2}$; $2 - 1 = \underline{1}$; $4 - 1 = \underline{3}$; $5 - 2 = \underline{3}$; $5 - 5 = \underline{0}$; $3 - 0 = \underline{3}$
2. $4 - 1 = \underline{3}$; $5 - 2 = \underline{3}$; $3 - 3 = \underline{0}$; $3 - 2 = \underline{1}$; $5 - 0 = \underline{5}$; $1 - 1 = \underline{0}$; $2 - 0 = \underline{2}$; $5 - 3 = \underline{2}$; $5 - 4 = \underline{1}$; $4 - 0 = \underline{4}$; $4 - 2 = \underline{2}$; $2 - 1 = \underline{1}$; $4 - 3 = \underline{1}$; $5 - 1 = \underline{4}$; $4 - 4 = \underline{0}$; $1 - 0 = \underline{1}$; $3 - 1 = \underline{2}$; $5 - 5 = \underline{0}$; Brain Stretch: $5 - 1 - 2 = \underline{2}$; $4 - 1 - 2 = \underline{1}$

Subtracting from 0 to 10 pp. 61–63

1. Check that students colour the picture correctly. $5 - 2 = \underline{3}$; $9 - 6 = \underline{3}$; $1 - 0 = \underline{1}$; $4 - 2 = \underline{2}$; $6 - 1 = \underline{5}$; $3 - 2 = \underline{1}$; $6 - 4 = \underline{2}$; $4 - 3 = \underline{1}$; $6 - 3 = \underline{3}$; $6 - 0 = \underline{6}$; $9 - 5 = \underline{4}$; $3 - 1 = \underline{2}$; $7 - 5 = \underline{2}$; $5 - 4 = \underline{1}$; $5 - 5 = \underline{0}$; $7 - 4 = \underline{3}$; $7 - 6 = \underline{1}$; $2 - 1 = \underline{1}$ **2.** $6 - 2 = \underline{4}$; $8 - 6 = \underline{2}$; $10 - 5 = \underline{5}$; $10 - 2 = \underline{8}$; $9 - 2 = \underline{7}$; $3 - 3 = \underline{0}$; $10 - 9 = \underline{1}$; $3 - 0 = \underline{3}$; $7 - 1 = \underline{6}$; $8 - 4 = \underline{4}$; $9 - 3 = \underline{6}$; $6 - 5 = \underline{1}$; $10 - 7 = \underline{3}$; $4 - 4 = \underline{0}$; $6 - 2 = \underline{4}$; $7 - 2 = \underline{5}$; $4 - 1 = \underline{3}$; $5 - 1 = \underline{4}$; Brain Stretch: $10 - 6 - 1 = \underline{3}$; $10 - 5 - 2 = \underline{3}$ **3.** $5 - 0 = \underline{5}$; $9 - 7 = \underline{2}$; $6 - 6 = \underline{0}$; $10 - 4 = \underline{6}$; $8 - 2 = \underline{6}$; $10 - 3 = \underline{7}$; $10 - 8 = \underline{2}$; $4 - 0 = \underline{4}$; $6 - 3 = \underline{3}$; $10 - 1 = \underline{9}$; $8 - 5 = \underline{3}$; $2 - 0 = \underline{2}$; $7 - 3 = \underline{4}$; $10 - 6 = \underline{4}$; $5 - 3 = \underline{2}$; $9 - 8 = \underline{1}$; $8 - 3 = \underline{5}$; $7 - 7 = \underline{0}$

Subtracting from 0 to 20 p. 64

1. $9 - 4 = \underline{5}$; $14 - 2 = \underline{12}$; $12 - 8 = \underline{4}$; $11 - 5 = \underline{6}$; $13 - 2 = \underline{11}$; $10 - 0 = \underline{10}$; $13 - 1 = \underline{12}$; $11 - 6 = \underline{5}$; $15 - 2 = \underline{13}$; $20 - 3 = \underline{17}$; $18 - 9 = \underline{9}$; $16 - 2 = \underline{14}$; $11 - 4 = \underline{7}$; $16 - 8 = \underline{8}$; $12 - 9 = \underline{3}$; $18 - 8 = \underline{10}$; $14 - 7 = \underline{7}$; $12 - 6 = \underline{6}$; $20 - 10 = \underline{10}$; $15 - 4 = \underline{11}$

Story Problems pp. 65–66

1. $8 - 3 = 5$; $7 - 4 = 3$; $9 - 3 = 6$ **2.** $6 - 2 = 4$; $3 - 1 = 2$; $5 - 4 = 1$

Subtraction Sentence Match p. 67

1. A line drawn from the subtraction sentence to the answer: 12 – 6, 6; 7 – 3, 4; 10 – 2, 8; 6 – 5, 1; 9 – 6, 3; 5 – 3, 2; 9 – 4, 5;
8 – 1, 7; 10 – 1, 9; 11 – 0, 11; 1 – 1, 0; 10 – 0, 10

Equal Parts p. 68

1. A circle drawn around each shape that shows one half:  Check that one half is
coloured.

Colouring One Half p. 69

1. 1 shape coloured green; 2 shapes coloured red; 4 shapes coloured blue; 3 shapes coloured green; 5 shapes coloured red;
6 shapes coloured blue

Naming the Fraction p. 70

1. A circle drawn around the correct fraction: $\frac{1}{3}$; $\frac{1}{2}$; $\frac{1}{3}$; $\frac{1}{4}$; $\frac{1}{2}$; $\frac{1}{3}$; $\frac{1}{4}$; $\frac{1}{4}$; $\frac{1}{4}$; $\frac{1}{3}$; $\frac{1}{2}$

Repeating Patterns pp. 71–72

1. Check that students extend the pattern.

2. Check that students extend the pattern.

Using Letters to Name Patterns p. 73

1. AB pattern: ABB pattern: Student patterns will vary. Example: ABA pattern

Creating Patterns p. 74

1. Check that students colour each pattern correctly and circle the core. Examples: red blue; green red pink;

blue blue red; red blue blue brown

Example of changing size: ABC pattern □ □ □

Example of changing position: ABC pattern

What Comes Next? p. 75

1. Check that students colour each pattern and extend the pattern correctly.

2D Shapes p. 76

1. Students connect the dots and draw each shape.

Matching 2D Shapes p. 77

1. A line drawn from the shape to its name: (in order of the shapes) rectangle, circle, triangle, square, hexagon, pentagon

What 2D Shapes Do You Know? p. 78

1. rectangle: 4 sides, 4 corners; circle: 0 sides, 0 corners; triangle: 3 sides, 3 corners; square: 4 sides, 4 corners;
rhombus: 4 sides, 4 corners; pentagon: 5 sides, 5 corners

Drawing Shapes p. 79

1. Check that students include the following shapes in their picture: rectangle, circle, triangle, and square.

Sorting 2D Shapes p. 80

1. Check that students correctly colour the shapes for each rule. Shapes with corners: rectangle, triangle, hexagon; shapes
with less than 4 sides: triangle, equilateral triangle; shapes with more than 3 sides: square, rectangle, hexagon; shapes with
more than 3 corners: square, hexagon

Symmetry p. 81

1. Check that students draw the line of symmetry accurately for each shape:

Drawing a Symmetrical Shape p. 82

1. Check that students' drawing shows both sides with the same shape and size.

Matching 3D Objects p. 83

1. A line drawn from the object to a similar item: (in order of the objects) sphere (ball); cube (die); pyramid (pyramid); cone (ice cream cone); cylinder (can); rectangular prism (gift box)

Sorting 3D Objects p. 84

1. Check that students correctly circle the object for each rule. objects that roll: cylinder, sphere; objects that cannot roll: prism, pyramid, cube; objects that can stack: cube, cylinder, prism; objects that cannot stack: cone, sphere

Following Directions pp. 85

1. Check that students correctly colour the picture according to the directions.

The Hour Hand p. 86

1. A line drawn between the same times: 7 o'clock and 7:00; 6:00 and 6 o'clock; 1 o'clock and 1:00; 12:00 and 12 o'clock

2. 8 o'clock or 8:00; 10 o'clock or 10:00; 6 o'clock or 6:00; 1 o'clock or 1:00

The Minute Hand p. 87

1. 9:00 or 9 o'clock; 9:30 or half past 9; 7:30 or half past 7; 1:30 or half past 1

Telling Time to the Hour p. 88

1. Check that students colour the hour hand blue and the minute hand red. 3 o'clock; 10 o'clock; 5 o'clock; 1 o'clock; 2 o'clock; 11 o'clock; 6 o'clock; 12 o'clock; 8 o'clock; 4 o'clock; 7 o'clock; 9 o'clock

Showing the Time to the Hour p. 89

1. Check that students draw 2 hands on the clock and colour the hour hand blue and the minute hand red.

Bed times will vary. Example: 8:30

Telling Time to the Half Hour p. 90

1. Check that students colour the hour hand blue and the minute hand red. 5; 10; 11; 8; 4; 7; 3; 2; 12; 9, 1, 6

What Time Is It? p. 91

A circle around the correct time: 4:00; 10:30; 3:30; 11:00; 3:00; 8:00; 7:30; 5:00; 12:30; 2:00; 4:30; 9:30

Time Match p. 92

A line drawn from the clock to the time (in order of the clocks): 4:00; 11:00; 7:30; 2:00

Canadian Coins p. 93

1. nickel; dime; quarter; loonie; toonie

Getting to Know Coins p. 94–95

1. A line drawn from the coin to its value and and its name: 100 cents, image of loonie, loonie; 25 cents, image of quarter, quarter; 5 cents, image of nickel, nickel; 200 cents, image of toonie, toonie; 10 cents, image of dime, dime

2. Check that students circle the coins correctly. Brain Stretch: 6 loonies; 13 nickels; 10 dimes; 11 quarters; 6 toonies

Adding Coins p. 96

1. 10 cents; 20 cents; 20 cents; 20 cents; 15 cents

Subtracting Coins p. 97

1. 5 cents; 10 cents; 5 cents; 5 cents; Brain Stretch: Look for a drawing of 2 nickels + 1 more nickel, 15¢; Look for a drawing of 3 nickels with 1 nickel crossed out, 10¢

Counting Nickels p. 98

1. 5¢, 10¢, 15¢, = 15¢; 5¢, 10¢, 15¢, 20¢, 25¢, 30¢, = 30¢; 5¢, 10¢, 15¢, 20¢, 25¢, = 25¢; 5¢, 10¢, 15¢, 20¢, = 20¢; 5¢, 10¢, 15¢, 20¢, 25¢, 30¢, 35¢, = 35¢

Counting Dimes p. 99

1. 10¢, 20¢, 30¢, 40¢, = 40¢; 10¢, 20¢, 30¢, 40¢, 50¢, 60¢, = 60¢; 10¢, 20¢, = 20¢; 10¢, 20¢, 30¢, 40¢, 50¢, 60¢, 70¢, = 70¢; Brain Stretch: 2; a drawing of 1 dime and 2 nickels and an addition sentence, 5¢ + 5¢ = 10¢

Candy Counter p. 100

1. 15¢; 20¢; 10¢; 15¢; 25¢,

Exploring Tally Charts p. 101

1. 10 children **2.** 8 children **3.** 4 children **4.** vanilla **5.** strawberry

Exploring Tally Charts p. 102

1. 9 blue **2.** 4 green **3.** red **4.** 16 **5.** blue, red, purple, green

Exploring Pictographs p. 103

1. 4 children **2.** 8 children **3.** 6 children **4.**

Exploring Pictographs p. 104

1. 7 children **2.** 5 children **3.** 3 children **4.**

Exploring Bar Graphs p. 105

1. 5, 3, 8 **2.**   **3.**

Exploring Bar Graphs p. 106

1. 5 ; 2 ; 4 - **2.** **3.**

Exploring Graphs p. 107

1.   **2.**

Comparing Height p. 108

1. 2, 1, 3; 2, 3, 1; 1, 2, 3; 2, 3, 1

Tallest to Shortest p. 106

1. 2, 1, 3; 2, 3, 1; 1, 2, 3; 2, 3, 1

Exploring Measuring with Non-standard Units p. 109

1. . 4 stars; 6 stars; 7 stars; 9 stars

Exploring Centimetres p. 110

1. 4 centimetres; 3 centimetres; 6 centimetres; 7 centimetres

Exploring Mass p. 111

1. 4 blocks; 15 blocks; 12 blocks; 3 blocks **2.** 2 more blocks on the left; 5 more blocks on the right; 3 more blocks on the left; 2 more blocks on the right; 6 more blocks on the right; 1 more block on the left; 1 more block on the right; 2 more blocks on the left